*The Best
Overnight
Hikes in
the Great
Smoky
Mountains*

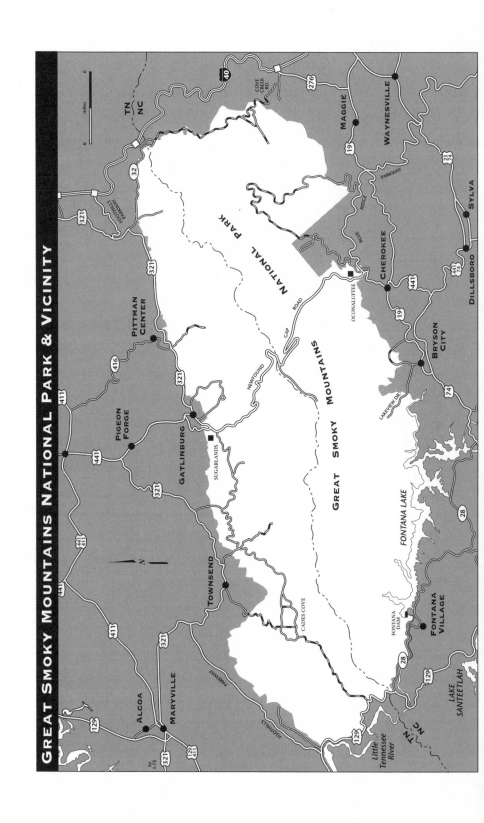

GREAT SMOKY MOUNTAINS NATIONAL PARK & VICINITY

The Best Overnight Hikes in the Great Smoky Mountains

James Andrews
and Kenneth Wise

The University of Tennessee Press / Knoxville

Copyright © 1997 by The University of Tennessee Press/ Knoxville. All Rights Reserved. Manufactured in the United States of America. First Edition.

The paper in this book meets the minimum requirements of the American National Standard for Permanence of Paper for Printed Library Materials. ∞ The binding materials have been chosen for strength and durability.

♲ Printed on recycled paper.

Frontispiece. The Great Smoky Mountains National Park.

Map on page ii printed courtesy of the University of Tennessee Cartography Laboratory. All other maps are printed courtesy of Bill Nelson.

This book is intended only as a general guide for the Great Smoky Mountains natural areas and trails and is not a substitute for individual outdoor skills, including survival and route finding. Each visitor to the Great Smoky Mountains should possess those outdoor skills, or be accompanied by an individual who does, since the specific information provided herein has been compiled from a variety of sources and is subject to the ever-changing natural and human-made environment.

Library of Congress Cataloging-in-Publication Data

Andrews, James, 1945–
    The best overnight hikes in the Great Smoky Mountains / James Andrews and Kenneth Wise. — 1st ed.
    p. cm.
    ISBN 0-87049-972-6 (pbk. : alk. paper)
    1. Hiking—Great Smoky Mountains (N.C. and Tenn.)—Guidebooks. 2. Great Smoky Mountains (N.C. and Tenn.)—Guidebooks. I. Wise, Kenneth, 1950– . II. Title.
GV199.42.G73A53 1997
796.5'1'0976889—dc21   96-45800
                                         CIP

Contents

Illustrations

FIGURES

MAPS

Introduction

The Great Smoky Mountains National Park is five hundred thousand acres of mountains, streams, and valleys straddling the Tennessee–North Carolina border where visitors can enjoy a wide variety of outdoor experiences. Perhaps the best way to experience these mountains is to spend the night in the backcountry. The large number of maintained trails offer mountain or streamside hikes of varying length and difficulty. Overnight camping on these trails allows visitors to reach the more remote regions of the Park and greatly increases the opportunities for observing the indigenous wildlife in its natural environment.

The Smoky Mountains are part of the Unaka Range, a subset of the Appalachian Mountains. As a group, they are the tallest mountains east of the Mississippi River with 14 peaks over 6,000 feet. Clingmans Dome, at 6,643 feet, is the highest mountain in the Park. Its neighbor, Mount Le Conte, is actually taller, meaning there is a greater elevation change from its base at Gatlinburg to its summit. In fact, Mount Le Conte is the tallest mountain east of the Mississippi River, while Clingmans Dome is the highest mountain along the Appalachian Trail.

The creation of the Park was a joint effort by conservationists, state and federal legislatures, and local government. After considerable effort, Congress passed a bill in 1926 which allowed the federal government to take possession of the Park once Tennessee and North Carolina had secured 150,000 acres. At the time that the two states set out to obtain land, there were over 7,000 people living in villages and farms on what is now Park land. In addition, over a dozen timber companies owned large tracts of land throughout the Smokies.

Congress formally authorized the Park in 1934, even though the Civilian Conservation Corps had started work on improvements several years earlier. President Franklin Roosevelt finally dedicated the Great Smoky Mountain National Park in a ceremony at Newfound Gap in 1940.

The Cherokees were the only residents in the Smokies when white settlers first started to arrive in the eighteenth century. While they ranged throughout these mountains, the Cherokees made their homes in villages alongside major mountain streams and rivers. A series of broken treaties and repressive legislation finally resulted in the removal of most of the remaining Cherokee population in 1838. These hapless people were marched to Oklahoma along the infamous Trail of Tears. Some Cherokees fled into the mountains and were later able to buy back some of their forfeited land. This area is now called the Qualla Reservation and lies along the North Carolina edge of the Park.

After the Cherokees had been removed, a hearty breed of pioneers gradually settled in areas once inhabited by the Cherokees. Those first settlers found a virtual paradise of dense forests, teeming with wild game, fish, berries, and honey. The sparse crops they raised were used to augment their diet. Eventually, however, settlements sprang up in the more hospitable regions, such as Cades Cove, Greenbrier, Cataloochee, and Sugarlands. Larger towns had to wait until the growing nation's need for lumber and building materials brought the lumber industry to the Smokies. When the lumber companies left, these mountains had been stripped of much of their forests.

Fortunately, because of moderate southern temperatures and abundant rainfall, the Smokies are once again covered with vegetation and seemingly overrun with wildlife. While some species, such as elk, cougar, and bison, are gone from the Park, there are still over seventy mammals found in these mountains. In addition to smaller mammals, such as squirrels, chipmunks, and groundhogs, hikers may also spot larger animals, including deer, and especially lucky hikers may observe a bear, coyote, red wolf, or, rarest of all, a bobcat.

White-tailed deer are abundant in these mountains, and, if you hike quietly, you are almost certain to see them on any extended hike. Since all hunting is prohibited in the Park, many deer have lost their fear of humans and will often remain even when they hear people approaching. This is particularly true for the Cades Cove area, where the deer leave the forest cover to graze, much like cattle, in the open meadows.

Extremely fortunate hikers may get to see the "top dog" in the Park, the American black bear. These shy creatures will almost always leave the area if they hear hikers coming. So, encounters are relatively rare, especially for those hiking in a group. Black bears are much smaller than their western cousin, the grizzly. No one should avoid the backcountry because of black bears. Bear attacks on humans are almost unheard of and rarely occur when people are not feeding them. Bears, it seems, do not understand when someone tells them that the food is all gone.

When not denned up for the winter, the black bear is an eating machine that needs to gain enough weight to see it through the winter months. Gaining weight can literally mean life or death for these magnificent creatures. In years where there is a late spring freeze and the acorn crop fails, bears may have to leave their dens early in search of food. Those that wander out of the Park are often killed on the surrounding highways. This is just one reason why visitors in the summer should not pick the wild berries found along the trails. Berries, nuts, rodents, and just about anything else that can be digested are vital to a healthy bear population.

The only other large mammals in the Park are river otters, bobcats, coyotes, foxes, red wolves, and wild boar. All are very shy and not likely to be encountered by hikers. The wild boar were imported from Europe and escaped from a game preserve in North Carolina. Boars root for food at night and do a great deal of damage to the forest floor and the roots of trees. The Park Service runs an ongoing boar eradication program, and hikers will often encounter the big rectangular wire traps used to catch them.

Cougars used to live in the Smokies, and, while there are often alleged sightings, the only hard evidence indicates that they are now extinct in this range. Eastern bison and elk are also gone from the Smokies. There is an ongoing attempt to reintroduce the red wolf begun in the early 1990s, and the river otter was successfully reintroduced in the late 1980s.

The forests in these mountains are seemingly layered with trees up and down the slopes. Cove hardwoods of sugar maple, basswood, silverbell, American beech, tulip poplar, buckeye, and red maple stand in the bottomland and on the lower flanks of the mountains. Clear-cutting was employed extensively in the lower elevations, and, even today, an area that was stripped of all its trees is recognizable by the almost uniform diameter of all the larger trees that have replaced those that were logged

Hemlock forests with an association of rhododendron and mountain laurel cover the banks of streams as they emerge from the cove hardwood forests. Since hemlock wood was of virtually no use to the lumber companies that decimated these mountains, very large hemlocks are frequently found alongside the mountain streams in the Park. Up until the early 1990s, dogwoods were also abundant in these forests. During those years, an imported fungus, which thrives in cool, moist regions, virtually wiped out the dogwood population in these mountains. Drier, sunny areas in this belt, like the tops of ridge lines, support a variety of oak trees and pines. Shaded and protected areas in this mid-zone contain forests comprising mostly birch and beech trees.

Spruce and Fraser fir trees dominate the highest peaks. This association, abundant in Canadian mountains, is unique to the Smokies in the United States. Unfortunately, an imported parasite has killed most of the large Fraser firs, and, where huge evergreens once stood, the mountain tops are now home to a sea of dead and graying tree trunks. Additionally, there is some evidence that the health of the spruce trees is dependent on the Fraser firs. Consequently, the spruce are showing signs of stress.

The dominant tree species in the Smokies was the American chestnut. Because it blossomed later in the spring and avoided late frosts, it was a very reliable source of food for the bear population and other animals dependent on a good crop of nuts. Unfortunately, the chestnut trees were wiped out in the 1920s and 1930s by an exotic fungus imported into this country around the turn of the century. Efforts to develop a resistant variety of the American chestnut have so far proved unsuccessful.

Occasionally, a peak will be covered in either grass or shrubs rather than trees. These peaks are known as balds, and their origins remain a mystery. Since they are prime grazing areas, eastern bison and elk probably kept them "mowed." When settlers arrived from North Carolina, cattle and sheep took over the job. Today, with neither wild nor domestic animals to fight them off, the surrounding forests are slowly erasing most of the balds.

Despite all the problems, however, the Smokies are quite resilient. The various blights and parasites only make room for new species to take the place of the old. With luck, future generations will enjoy backcountry hikes almost identical to those described in this book. The hikes we have included will take visitors to the most beautiful and readily accessible places in the Park, areas that are truly worth seeing over and over again.

PREPARING FOR A BACKCOUNTRY HIKE

Permits

Permits are free and conveniently obtained. The Park Service requires all overnight campers to have a backcountry permit in their possession when they camp in the Park. The Service uses a simple self-registration system that merely requires campers to fill in the permit form available at all Park entrances. For campsites that require reservations, simply call the Backcountry Registration Office at (423) 436-1231. A copy of the permit you fill out remains at the Park entrance, and, for everyone's safety and convenience, you should stick to the itinerary you list on your permit.

Preparation

We always take reasonable precautions, even though there is little to present a significant risk on these trails. You literally have a better chance of being struck by lightning than getting attacked by a bear, bitten by a snake, or getting lost on these trails. That said, here is some information that might make your hike more pleasant:

1. Wear sturdy, stiff soled shoes which provide good ankle support. There are loose rocks on every trail and a good pair of hiking boots is the best way to avoid a sprained ankle.

2. If there is more than one in your party, spread the load. There is no need for everyone to bring a camp stove or a water filter. When we take a one night hike, we bring the following "communal" items. A) A small grill or rack from a barbecue or an old microwave. These are very light and can be tied on the outside of a back pack. B) About a dozen self-lighting charcoal briquettes. C) Some fresh croissants, bagels, muffins, or other breakfast bread. D) One camp stove for every two hikers. E) If we are not camping at a shelter, one lightweight tarpaulin (to provide cover from the rain). F) One water filter. G) Two pots for boiling liquids and one frying pan. H) Plenty

of toilet paper. I) A repair kit with at least: patches for a leaky tent or air mattress; a couple of large needles; strong nylon thread; replacement pins and wire loops for external frame packs; strong safety pins; small needle-nose pliers or an all purpose repair tool. J) A couple of large water containers or water bags (nothing is more tedious than endless trips from the campsite to the water source). K) Insect repellent.

3. Each person in the party should have a good whistle readily available while hiking. This is more effective and less exhausting than shouting for one another in the unlikely event you become separated. It will also generally terrify and chase off an overly aggressive bear.

4. Take good food. On an overnight hike, you only have to carry food for, at most, four meals: lunch and dinner for the first half and breakfast and lunch for the next day. Pack weight is not normally a problem if you spread items equally among your party. We have tried the freeze-dried food, and grilled steaks are definitely better. You can preserve your food by freezing some of your drinking water in a strong ziplock bag or in a plastic bottle and carrying it in a plastic bag with your perishables. The large chunk of ice will keep steaks fresh for grilling. You can also freeze egg substitutes for breakfast omelets and use them as a coolant for your other foods.

Park Rules

1. You can only camp at a designated site or shelter.
2. Park rules limit your party to eight persons or less.
3. For toilet use, walk at least one hundred feet from the trail, while glancing back to be certain of the trail's location. Be sure you are well away from a water source or campsite and then dig a hole at least six inches deep using a shovel or the heel of your boot. Cover the hole with dirt when you are finished.
4. Bag all trash, including tampons and sanitary napkins, and haul it out with you. You can burn empty tin cans in your campfire to remove the odor and avoid attracting bears. Just be sure to bag them as well and take them out.
5. Do not pick or cut flowers, berries, trees, or other foliage. Remember, some bears do not make it through the winter because there were not enough blueberries, blackberries, and edible plants for them in the summer.
6. Do not feed the wildlife. Animals that learn to rely on humans for food are doomed in the winter when there is no one around to feed them.
7. If they are available, store your food in bear lockers. If not, hang food and trash on a line suspended at least ten feet off the ground, with the nearest limb or tree trunk at least five feet from the bag.
8. Do not cut trees for firewood. Collect dead wood from the ground for your campfire.

Precautions

There are only a few realistic backpacking dangers. The most life threatening is hypothermia. Storms and sudden temperature drops can occur very quickly in these mountains. Always carry a poncho or a rain suit. Either will keep you dry and hold in body heat. Also be sure to carry a dry change of clothing in a ziplock bag. We also leave a dry change in the car so that, no matter what happens, we do not have to drive home wearing wet clothes.

Other problems that befall hikers with some frequency are sprained ankles and twisted knees. This frequently occurs when someone slips on a rock while crossing a stream. If a stream crossing looks particularly difficult, take off your boots and wade it. Wading is often quicker and easier than wandering around on the bank searching for those perfectly placed rocks.

Lastly, dehydration or heat exhaustion can become a problem for backpackers who do not drink enough water or take frequent rest stops. A handy way to keep cool is to wear a wet bandanna around your forehead. There are plenty of streams and springs in these mountains for rewetting, and, especially on a hot summer day, a bandanna can quickly become your favorite piece of equipment. There is no substitute, however, for drinking plenty of water.

First Aid

1. Bring along a well-equipped first aid kit.
2. Snake bite is a rare event in these mountains. In fact, there has never been a fatality from a snake bite in the Park. All snakes try to avoid human contact, and encounters, especially with poisonous snakes, seldom occur. As a precaution, however, carry an inexpensive snake bite kit (available in any outdoor store) and follow the included instructions in the unlikely event someone is bitten.
3. Blisters, however, are not rare. Wear two pair of socks and bring plenty of mole skin. Stop at the first sign of irritation and put mole skin on the affected area.
4. Surprisingly, insect bites and bee stings account for the majority of medical emergencies in the Park, so plan accordingly.

We always adhere to the precautions we have suggested. It gives us a secure feeling when we hike that we will be prepared for any emergency. These mountains, because of the relatively low altitude and the good condition of the trails, are very safe for backpacking. The ten overnight hikes in this book represent a challenging yet enjoyable way for hikers to get to know most of the major backcountry regions in this wonderful wilderness.

The Best
Overnight
Hikes in
the Great
Smoky
Mountains

Big Creek

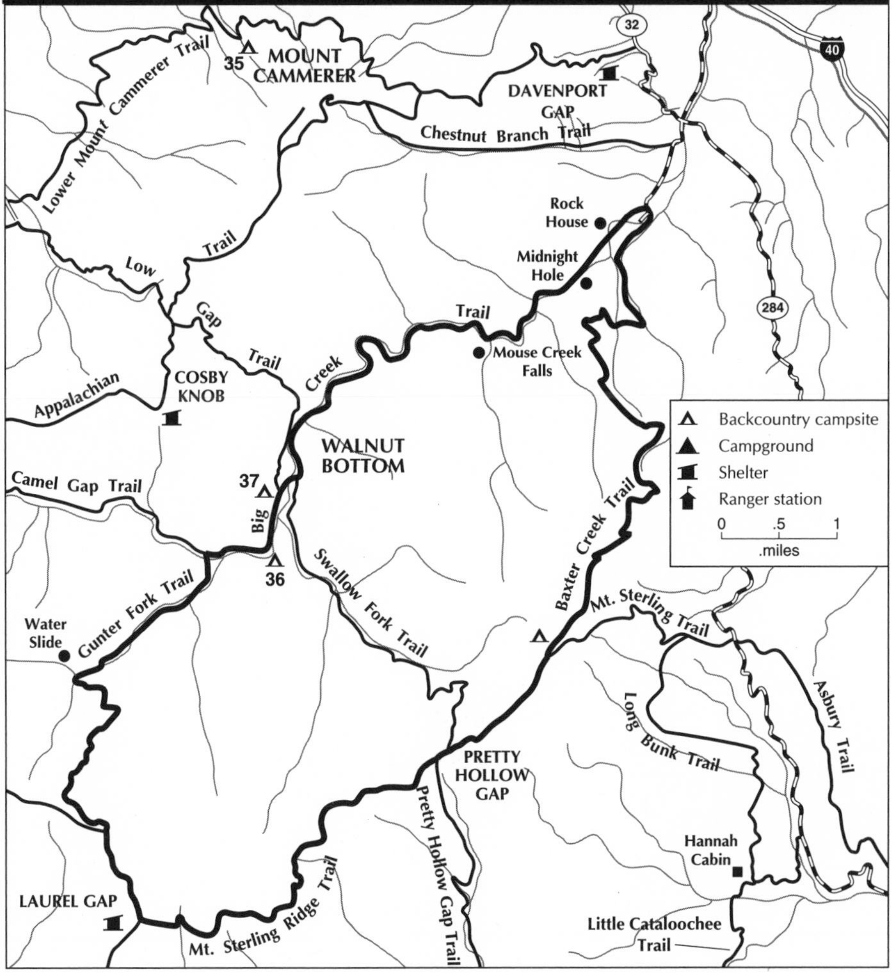

35
MOUNT CAMMERER
Lower Mount Cammerer Trail
32
40
DAVENPORT GAP
Chestnut Branch Trail
Low Gap Trail
Rock House
Midnight Hole
284
Trail
Big Creek Trail
Mouse Creek Falls
Appalachian
COSBY KNOB
WALNUT BOTTOM
37
Camel Gap Trail
36
Swallow Fork Trail
Baxter Creek Trail
Mt. Sterling Trail
Water Slide
Gunter Fork Trail
Long Bunk Trail
Asbury Trail
PRETTY HOLLOW GAP
Pretty Hollow Gap Trail
Hannah Cabin
LAUREL GAP
Mt. Sterling Ridge Trail
Little Cataloochee Trail
Backcountry campsite
Campground
Shelter
Ranger station
0
.5
1
.miles

BIG CREEK

Big Creek Trail–Gunter Fork Trail–Balsam Mountain Trail–Mount Sterling Ridge Trail–Mount Sterling Trail–Baxter Creek Trail.

Distance: 23.3 miles round-trip.

Elevation gain: 4,050 feet.

Brief trail description: This is, overall, probably the best overnight loop in the Park. The hike includes several unique and impressive geological features, spectacular panoramic vistas, a powerful mountain stream, and a virgin forest.

How to get there: Take Interstate 40 and exit at Waterville (about halfway between Knoxville, Tennessee, and Asheville, North Carolina). There is an old brick power station sitting astride the Pigeon River. The road proceeds to the right about 2.7 miles straight through an intersection with old NC 284, past the Big Creek Ranger Station, and into the parking lot at Big Creek Campground.

Recommended campsite: Laurel Gap Shelter. (Reservations required.)

0.0—Big Creek Road.

1.0—Rock House.

1.4—Midnight Hole.

2.0—Mouse Creek Falls.

2.8—Brakeshoe Spring.

5.2—Walnut Bottom. Swallow Fork Trail leads left 4.0 miles to Mount Sterling Ridge at Pretty Hollow Gap.

5.4—Backcountry campsite 37. Low Gap Trail leads right 2.5 miles to the Appalachian Trail at Low Gap.

5.7—Backcountry campsite 36.

5.8—Camel Gap Trail leads straight 4.8 miles to the Appalachian Trail at Camel Gap.

6.4—Gunter Fork Trail leads left 4.1 miles to the Balsam Mountain Trail.

6.5—Difficult crossing of Big Creek.

7.8—Gunter Fork Cascade.

8.2—Water slide.

10.5—Balsam Mountain Trail leads left 1.1 miles to the Laurel Gap Shelter.

11.4—Mount Sterling Ridge Trail leads left 5.3 miles to the Mount Sterling Trail. Laurel Gap Shelter lies 300 yards farther down the Balsam Mountain Trail.

16.7—Mount Sterling Trail leads left 0.4 mile to backcountry campsite 38.

17.1—Mount Sterling firetower. Backcountry campsite 38. Baxter Creek Trail leads 6.2 miles to the Big Creek picnic grounds.

23.3—Big Creek Road.

This loop provides one of the best overnight hiking and camping experiences in the Park. The hike itself is interesting and varied from beginning to end with lots of water, scenic overlooks, second-growth hardwoods, unique geological features, and a majestic, uncut forest for a finale. Big Creek itself is one of the most picturesque streams in the Smokies, and the breathtaking view from the Mount Sterling firetower is well worth the climb. As for the accommodations, uncrowded Laurel Gap Shelter is the most comfortable, hospitable, and unspoiled of all the Park's shelters.

The entire hike consists of a loop, beginning and ending at the Big Creek parking lot. The Big Creek Trail leaves the lower edge of the parking lot on the opposite side of the lot from the stream. It immediately gains moderate elevation as it knifes through a narrow, walled opening where the stream escapes from the watershed.

This entrance is the start of the six-mile Big Creek Trail into a magnificent basin surrounded by 3,000-foot peaks and forested ridges. The trail, which is really an abandoned logging railroad bed for the first six miles, is the easiest imaginable way to gain the first thousand feet of elevation on this loop. In addition to the gentle grade, the trail is sure and easy on the feet.

The stream and the floor of the basin are strewn with boulders which, in both size and number, are unequaled anywhere else in the Park. About one mile into the hike, a steep path leaves the right side of the trail and climbs for about two hundred feet to a unique geological feature known as the Rock House. Here, nature has stacked massive boulders upon one another in varying configurations. One set has

Midnight Hole on Big Creek. Courtesy of Lou A. Murray.

virtually perpendicular "walls" and a flat, thirty-foot-high "ceiling." This creates a giant room which provided temporary shelter for early settlers as they built more traditional cabins.

One mile up, the trail skirts Midnight Hole, named for the deep, dark emerald green color of the pool at the foot of a ten-foot waterfall. The fall forms when the stream is squeezed through a slit in the rocks just before it drops into a large, twelve-foot-deep pool. The water is extremely clear and of a rich color unique to several pools spaced along Big Creek.

A half mile above Midnight Hole, Mouse Creek cascades fifty feet down the face of a rocky cliff on the far side of Big Creek. Actually, several individual streamlets descend irregularly to an unused logging road where they gather for a final ten-foot drop to Big Creek. The delicate waterfall, framed as it is by the green mountainside on the far side of the creek, is actually more refreshing than powerful in appearance.

About a quarter of a mile above Mouse Creek Falls, the trail shoots across a sturdy bridge spanning yet another of the ubiquitous pools adorning Big Creek. The trail and creek prowl the gorge side by side for the next two miles, making the rushing stream a welcome companion to the hike. This association of trail and stream affords unlimited opportunities to drop off the trail and explore the rocky creek.

About a half mile above the bridge crossing, a small but relatively well-known spring cascades over a mossy stone to the left of the trail. Earlier in the century, an engineer from a logging train placed a locomotive brakeshoe on the rock just below the spring to capture the water. Passersby soon named the spot Brakeshoe Spring, and the substantial iron shoe remained in its place for fifty years until some unthinking souvenir hunter filched it sometime in the mid-1970s.

About three miles above Brakeshoe Spring, the trail is marked by the lower terminus of the Swallow Fork Trail near the entrance to Walnut Bottoms, a way station on the old railroad line. Two hundred yards past this junction, the trail crosses a bridge and passes the first of two very hospitable, scenic campsites almost adjacent to each other along the stream. Just beyond the first site the Low Gap Trail forks right on its way across the mountain to the Cosby Campground.

This campsite—like others in the Park—is sometimes closed because of bear activity. This precautionary measure is usually taken when bears have become too habituated to human contact. A ranger related to us a story about two fishermen who had come to the Park for a weekend of fly fishing. They had spent the day in the stream and were sleeping in the shell on the back of their pickup truck. It was a hot summer night, and they left the tailgate open to get some air. The two fell asleep with an open bag of corn chips between them. They were awakened by a bear standing on top of them with its head in the bag of chips. Neither the bear nor the fishermen were injured. The bear, however, was the more endangered because the experience helped habituate it to human contact and human food.

About a mile from its juncture with the Low Gap Trail, the Big Creek Trail fades into the Camel Gap Trail. A quick exit left puts the hiker onto the Gunter Fork Trail, which immediately fords Big Creek and begins an initially lazy ascent up the mountain. Generally, a hiker has to bite the bullet and wade the calf-deep stream at this point. One note of caution about the Gunter Fork Trail: because of the nature of this watershed, the trail crossing can become deep and hazardous after heavy rains or thundershowers.

On the far side of Big Creek, the trail forces the hiker to rock-hop several times as it crisscrosses Gunter Fork. About a mile and a half from the trailhead, at a sharp left turn in the trail, a path leads right and downhill to the Gunter Fork Cascades, a ten-foot drop by Gunther Fork over a cliff edge into a waist-deep pool.

About five hundred yards and a couple of easy stream crossings farther along, the trail passes the base of a two-hundred-foot water slide. This is truly an impressive piece of rock. At the top, a thin sheet of water slides over a dome-shaped edge and drops twenty feet onto this very long water slide. A thin film of water then makes the long slide into a small pool beside the trail.

Just beyond this point, the trail crosses the stream a final time before starting a fairly strenuous climb to Balsam Mountain. A half mile above this last crossing, there is a switchback to a cleared ridge point. A convenient opening to the left frames a panoramic view of the stateline divide near Cosby Knob. Most prominent on the hillsides are the thick laurel slicks, or "hells," which hug the steep slopes descending the divide. Off-trail hikers will recognize these as almost impassable obstacles and can readily agree about the appropriateness of the colloquial term.

A second overlook, with a good view of the Gunter Fork watershed and Sevenmile Beech Ridge, follows closely on the heels of the first. Beyond these overlooks, the trail degenerates into a rocky berm that hugs the steep slopes of the mountain. In summer, weeds and undergrowth may occasionally obscure parts of the path. The hardwoods give way to red spruce about a half mile from the crest as the trail levels out for a fairly easy climb to the intersection with the Balsam Mountain Trail.

The route takes you left on the Balsam Mountain Trail for an uneventful one-mile hike along the spine of an overgrown ridge line down to Laurel Gap. The trail is well worn and rocky, clearly the victim of horse traffic. Turn right where the Mount Sterling Ridge Trail intersects and pick your way three hundred yards along the eroded trail to the only five-star "hotel" in the Smokies, the Laurel Gap Shelter.

This little-used shelter is nestled among the trees in a grassy clearing that becomes weedy by late summer. There is a very reliable water source about two hundred yards beyond the shelter, and, most important, there is a picnic table. Veteran hikers and campers know what a luxury it is, after several hours of hauling a pack up and down the mountains, to actually sit upright at a table and eat supper.

Because it is located off the Appalachian Trail, the site has a more pristine look about it than the areas surrounding the more frequently used Appalachian Trail shelters. Often a camping party will find it has the shelter to itself; except, of course, for the hummingbirds that frequent the little clearing in mid- to late summer and the deer that visit at dusk and dawn.

To start home the next day, campers should retrace their way back one-third of a mile to the intersection with the Balsam Mountain Trail. Turn right on the Mount Sterling Ridge Trail to begin a leisurely, rolling, four-mile descent to Pretty Hollow Gap.

A number of former balds along this ridge are currently home to immature balsam forests. Today, these prime rooting sites for wild feral pigs are frequently found in plowed condition. The Cherokees believed the original balds to be the devil's footprints. The footprints led to the Devil's Bedchamber, the Cherokee name for Mount Sterling. For some unknown reason, the Devil's Bedchamber was renamed Mount Sterling in honor of an anonymous woodcutter from Sterling, Kentucky.

This entire length of trail was first used by Cherokees on hunting forays and then later by white settlers taking their cattle to and from grazing patches high in these mountains. Just before it enters Pretty Hollow Gap, the trail threads through a remarkably long and flat stand of beech trees. The light filtering through the leaves in the summer gives this stretch an almost cathedral-like appearance.

Pretty Hollow Gap itself opens nicely into a grassy, spongy clearing nestled in a pronounced saddle bisected by the Pretty Hollow Gap and the Swallow Fork Trails coming up opposite sides of the mountain. At this point the trail angles upward for a mile and one-half until it reaches the top of Mount Sterling. About fifty yards from the gap, a tall spruce stands right beside the trail. Burned into the tree from top to bottom is a scar from a lightning bolt from a recent thunderstorm—a perfect thirty-foot-long tattoo created in a split second.

Just prior to reaching Mount Sterling, the trail intersects the Mount Sterling Trail before it passes through a spacious campsite dotted liberally with small fir trees. A firetower sits atop the summit itself and, if it is a clear day, there is a spectacular 360 degree panoramic view available from its stairs. The Big Creek Basin is to the north, bounded by the eastern end of the Smoky Mountain Divide. Mount Cammerer is the sharp peak directly across the basin and Low Gap is the deep notch to its left. To the south, the view is into Cataloochee and to the Pisgah National Forest beyond. To the west, one can look down the stateline divide along the tallest peaks in the Appalachian chain.

Once the trail leaves the tower it begins a 4,100-foot descent through one of the finest and most diverse forests in the Smokies to return to the parking lot at the mouth of Big Creek. Initially, the trail passes through sparsely placed spruce surrounded by an endless supply of small fir trees. About five hundred yards from the top, a spur runs sharply downhill for seven hundred feet from the left side of the trail to the water source for the campsite atop Mount Sterling. This is a prolific little spring surrounded by touch-me-nots. The climb back to the trail is short but steep.

Shortly thereafter, the ridge line rises to the right, and the trail is separated from the crest by a magnificent stand of spruce and fir growing up from a carpet of moss-covered rocks. The air is filled with the pungent odor of the firs, and the vivid contrast in shades of green accented by the deep shadows of this boreal world literally assaults the eyes.

About two miles from the top and just before the junction with the Big Branch Trail, the forest makes a transition to a spruce-hemlock association. The size of the trees is living proof that loggers never plundered these steep slopes. Avoid the Big Branch Trail, as it is poorly maintained and, the last time we hiked it, there were many difficult blowdowns blocking the way. There is really more to recommend on the Baxter Creek Trail.

The trail continues to drop quickly through a spacious, secluded forest of stately hemlocks and gnarled old maples and beeches, with the red spruce gradually disappearing in the lower elevations. This portion of the trail is followed by a series of hikes from switchbacks out to ridge points and back again. The trail constantly loses elevation during this phase and is often shrouded with rhododendron. Lower down, Fraser magnolia, striped maple, blackgum, sassafras, sourwood, and Carolina silverbell begin to dominate.

Just before the trail drops into the bottomland, poplar, hickory, red maple, and flowering dogwood take over. The bottomland itself was both thoroughly logged and heavily settled. Various artifacts are still visible along the trail, and, just before the trail reaches the creek, a path shoots off to the left for a quarter mile to a massive, sixty-foot-high, stacked stone chimney, the remains of a large lodge that once stood on the banks of Big Creek.

The trail, through the bottomland, traces along the base of a high ridge. There is a rugged rock face above and the sound of the distant creek filters through the densely packed second-growth poplars that have overgrown the old homesteads. Just before reaching Big Creek, the Big Branch Trail rejoins the Baxter Creek Trail. There is a short but steep drop to a fragile-looking metal catwalk that funnels overnight hikers right back into the parking lot they left the day before. 🚶

CADES COVE

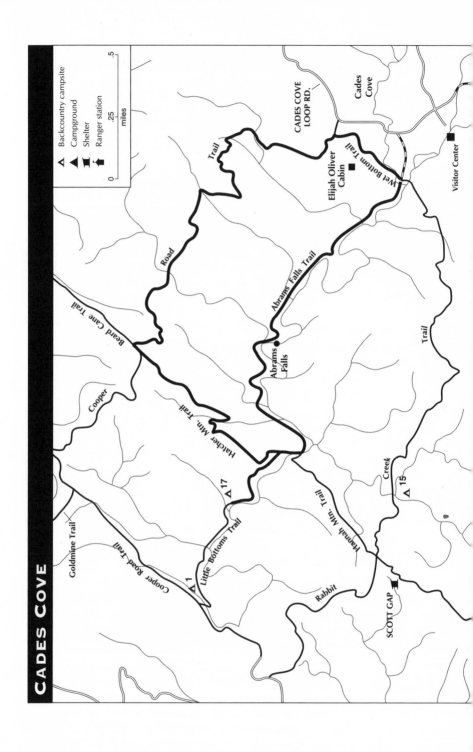

Backcountry campsite
Campground
Shelter
Ranger station

0   .25   .5
miles

Beard Cane Trail

Cooper

Road

Trail

Goldmine Trail

Cooper Road Trail

Little Bottoms Trail

Hatcher Mtn. Trail

▲ 17

▲ 1

Hannah Mtn. Trail

Rabbit

Creek

Trail

▲ 15

SCOTT GAP

Abrams Falls

Abrams Falls Trail

CADES COVE LOOP RD.

Elijah Oliver Cabin

Wet Bottom Trail

Cades Cove

Visitor Center

Abrams Falls Trail–Hatcher Mountain Trail–Little Bottoms Trail–Cooper Road Trail–Wet Bottom Trail.

Distance: 14.9 miles round-trip.

Elevation gain: 1,900 feet.

Brief trail description: This predominantly streamside and ridge hike includes a fine swimming hole, little uphill hiking, and one of the more hospitable campsites.

How to get there: To reach Cades Cove, enter the Park at Townsend, Tennessee, and drive one mile to the Townsend Wye where the Little River Road intersects the Laurel Creek Road. Turn right and drive 7.0 miles to the end of Laurel Creek Road. The Cades Cove Loop Road begins at the end of Laurel Creek Road. Drive along the one-way Cades Cove Loop Road 5.0 miles, turning right onto a gravel road that terminates within 0.5 mile at a parking area. The Abrams Falls Trail begins at the wooden bridge at the end of the parking area.

Recommended campsite: 17.

0.0—Cades Cove at the Abrams Falls parking area. Trail to the Elijah Oliver Place leads right at the far end of the bridge over Abrams Creek.

2.5—Abrams Falls.

4.2—Hatcher Mountain Trail leads right 0.2 mile to the Little Bottoms Trail and 2.8 miles to the Cooper Road Trail.

4.4—Little Bottoms Trail leads left 0.7 mile to back-country campsite 17.

5.1—Backcountry campsite 17.

5.8—Return to Hatcher Mountain Trail. Hatcher Mountain Trail leads left 2.6 miles to the Cooper Road Trail.

8.4—Cooper Road Trail leads right 5.5 miles to the Wet Bottom Trail and 5.7 miles to the Cades Cove Loop Road. Beard Cane Creek Trail leads straight 4.2 miles to the Ace Gap Trail.

13.9—Wet Bottom Trail leads right 1.0 mile to the Abrams Falls parking area.

14.2—Wet Bottom Trail turns left into lowland. Jeep track leads straight 200 yards to the Elijah Oliver Place.

14.9—Abrams Falls parking area.

Abrams Falls and the other trails in this hike are distributed around Cades Cove, a flat limestone basin four miles long and one mile wide that is surrounded by mountains. Thunderhead and the stateline divide are on the south, Rich Mountain is to the north, Bote Mountain is to the east, and Hatcher and Hannah Mountains stand guard on the west.

The hike begins with a drive through picture-perfect Cades Cove. This well-defined basin is drained by Abrams Creek, the largest stream whose course lies en-

Smoky Mountain black bear. Photograph courtesy of the National Park Service.

tirely within the Park. The Cades Cove Loop Road runs a lap around the cove and past several restored sites exhibiting nineteenth-century Appalachian architecture. Of particular interest are the John Oliver Cabin, the oldest log building in the cove, and Cables Mill, a remainder from the cove's industrial period. The loop road also passes cabins, barns, farms, churches, and cemeteries that were an integral part of the thriving settlement that once inhabited this fertile bottomland.

On the drive in, campers will almost certainly be able to spot white-tailed deer in the grassy meadowlands or in the edge of the woods along the loop road. Visitors may also encounter a traffic jam where motorists have spotted a black bear and have congregated to watch it. Bears in the Cades Cove area are often habituated to people and are therefore spotted more frequently. Most bears in the wild disappear when they hear hikers approaching.

The hike to Abrams Falls is a pleasant streamside walk along Abrams Creek, which is nourished by eighteen smaller streams that drain the slopes of the Cades Cove basin and feed into Abrams Creek as it winds westward through the center of the cove. The creek exits the cove through an aperture at the lower end, then winds its way down a narrow gorge to its mouth at Chilhowee Lake, near the southwest corner of the Park.

The name "Abrams" is a truncation of Abraham, erstwhile chief of the Cherokees. Chief Abram was known for leading the last Indian attacks on Watauga settlement. He presided over Chilhowee Village on the Little Tennessee near the mouth of what is now called Abrams Creek, hence the association of his name with the primary stream in Cades Cove.

Abrams Creek is one of the better trout streams in the Park, and the hiker will frequently see people fly fishing in its many pools. Surprisingly, fish form virtually none of the black bear's diet. Unlike its cousins, the grisly bear and the brown bear, the American black bear is a very poor hunter and is even less skilled at fishing. Instead, black bears depend mainly on browsing and scavenging. As a case in point, we have a friend who had spent the day fishing this creek and had managed to catch several nice-sized trout, which he had on a stringer at the water's edge. He was in the stream casting for that really big one, when he heard a noise behind him. He spun around just in time to see a bear disappearing into a rhododendron thicket with his fish. Bears may not be able to catch them, but there is almost nothing they would prefer over fish. As a matter of fact, the bear census in the Park is taken by hanging sardine cans from trees and calculating how often they are found and chewed up by bears.

The trail begins where Abrams Creek leaves Cades Cove and enters the mountain fastness. It crosses a bridge over a stream where it immediately intersects a connector leading in from the Elijah Oliver homeplace. The Abrams Falls Trail turns left at this junction and follows Abrams Creek four miles downstream, terminating at the Hannah Mountain Trail. Except for a brief hiatus while clearing Arbutus Ridge, the trail adheres to the bank of the creek. From the gap in Arbutus Ridge, Abrams Creek can be seen two hundred feet below as it enters the Big Horseshoe where the stream travels for nearly a mile, making almost a complete loop. The lower end of the ridge is a narrow neck separating the ends of the loop.

As the trail descends Arbutus Ridge, it returns to its streamside course at the lower end of the Big Horseshoe and continues, rising occasionally to clear another low ridge or two before descending to the mouth of Wilson Creek. Here a short side trail leads left to Abrams Falls.

At the falls, the placid, meandering Abrams Creek is shunted into a chute along the far side, transforming the stream into a raging torrent that fires over a ledge before it drops twenty feet into one of the largest natural pools in the Smokies. The closer edge of the falls is bounded by a rocky, double ledge, while the far end is framed by overhanging rhododendron and laurel that scale the steep outer bank of the creek. In hotter weather, sunbathers lie out on the lower ledge while enjoying refreshing dips into the dark green pool, whose bottom is lost in a gloom that obscures the clarity of its icy water.

The remaining two miles of the trail are more isolated and rugged than the prior section. The trail keeps to Abrams Creek, rising to clear some minor ridges that offer opportunities to look down and along the stream's rugged gorge. The trail terminates at the Abrams Creek Ford, marking the lower terminus of the Hannah Mountain and Hatcher Mountain Trails. The Hannah Mountain Trail fords Abrams Creek immediately to the left. The Hatcher Mountain Trail climbs right to the eastern terminus of the Little Bottoms Trail and then continues to the Cooper Road Trail.

Deer are particularly abundant in the Cades Cove area, and we saw the largest herd of them we had ever encountered at the Abrams Creek Ford. Early in the year, a group of about a dozen deer were browsing on the nearby foliage. Three of them were bucks in the process of shedding the spring velvet from their antlers. In this state, they seem to resemble walking clothes racks. Rather than flee into the woods, they merely noted our presence and walked slowly away from the trail.

The Hatcher Mountain Trail turns away from the stream and climbs 0.2 mile to the Little Bottom Trail, then along Hatcher Mountain to the intersection of the Beard Cane Creek Trail with the Cooper Road Trail. Turn at the Little Bottoms Trail and follow it for seven-tenths of a mile to campsite 17. Because it is so narrow, the Little Bottoms Trail was known to old-timers as "the goat trail." In places the path is little more than an etching not much wider than a hiking boot. When not climbing around a tree or a bit of root latticework, "the goat trail" is edging along stretches of rock ledge.

The Little Bottoms Trail rejoins the creek at the upper end of an extensive flat that was once a farm, and is now Little Bottoms Backcountry Campsite (17). The camp, situated on a small rise above Abrams Creek, is nearly thirty yards wide and extends seventy-five yards from front to back. Near the back of the site is a stone fence that remains from a farm that once stood here. These days the fence is home for an occasional copperhead. The site is exceptionally fine for camping, apart from the snakes, and it has the added amenity of an excellent swimming hole in the nearby creek. The visitor may well fall asleep to the sound of a babbling brook.

In the morning, retrace the Little Bottoms Trail to its junction with the Hatcher Mountain Trail. Turn left at the Hatcher Mountain Trail. The trail climbs out of the Abrams Creek gorge for a half mile before turning onto the crest of Hatcher Mountain.

Just prior to reaching the ridge line, the trail enters an enclosed hollow harboring Oak Flats Branch. Dense thickets of rhododendron range along the streamside, with hemlocks and white pine providing the forest cover.

From the Oak Flats drainage, the trail ascends to the spine of Hatcher Mountain and follows a delightful course through dry-ridge hardwoods and pines. The trail stays on the ridge until terminating in the Cooper Road Trail about one mile above the Oak Flats crossing.

At the crossing, the Beard Cane Trail is straight ahead, with the Cooper Road Trail running left to right. Go to the right (east) to return to Cades Cove. Cooper Road was once used extensively by herders driving cattle to graze on the upland ranges of the mountains. One such range, known locally as Yellow Sulfur, extended along the Cooper Road to the head of Beard Cane Trail. Unlike the ranges along the higher elevations, Yellow Sulfur was reclaimed quickly by the wilderness, leaving no traces of its former boundaries.

The Cooper Road Trail descends gradually to a rendezvous with Wilson Branch, a small, benign stream that marks the onset of the cool, damp conditions conducive to growing large hemlocks. The trail and stream proceed together for a short distance through a deep hollow that harbors a secluded enclave of these giants, which preside over an understory of thinly scattered rhododendron and mountain laurel. The trail soon returns to the drier environment, but will twice more repeat this cycle as it passes the Stony and Arbutus Branches.

Although the trail climbs and descends as it enters and leaves the creek hollows, it retains its wide, roadlike quality and never exceeds a moderate grade. For its final mile, the trail passes through a dry woodland that opens into the western end of Cades Cove. Just before the trail terminates in the Cades Cove Loop Road near the northwest corner of the cove, it is intersected from the right by the Wet Bottom Trail.

Wet Bottom Trail is a short (one-mile) connector with the Abrams Falls parking area. It starts with a pleasant quarter-mile hike down to a large red barn built by John W. Oliver. Turn right on the road running just in front of the barn. Shortly beyond the barn the Wet Bottom Trail exits left from the road. It is easier and drier to stay on the road to the Elijah Oliver Place, where the Park Service has preserved a post–Civil War farmstead. The farm itself is now woodland, but the farmhouse and its outbuildings are well maintained. From the Elijah Oliver Place, just follow the walkway a half mile back to the Abrams Falls Trailhead. 🏃

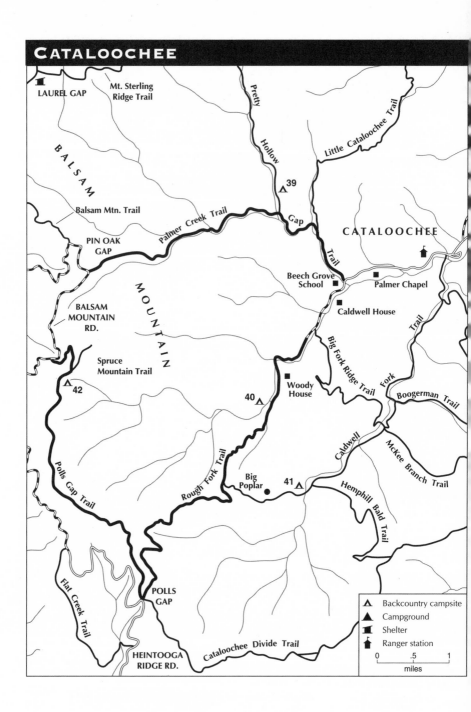

CATALOOCHEE

LAUREL GAP

Mt. Sterling
Ridge Trail

Pretty

Hollow

Little Cataloochee Trail

B A L S A M

Balsam Mtn. Trail

Palmer Creek Trail

Gap

△ 39

C A T A L O O C H E E

PIN OAK
GAP

Trail

Beech Grove
School ■

■ Palmer Chapel

M
O
U
N
T
A
I
N

BALSAM
MOUNTAIN
RD.

Caldwell House ■

Big Fork Ridge Trail

Fork

Trail

Spruce
Mountain Trail

△ 42

Woody ■
House

40 △

Boogerman Trail

Caldwell

McKee Branch Trail

Polls Gap Trail

Rough Fork Trail

Big
Poplar ●

41 △

Hemphill Bald Trail

POLLS
GAP

Flat Creek Trail

HEINTOOGA
RIDGE RD.

Cataloochee Divide Trail

△	Backcountry campsite
▲	Campground
■	Shelter
⛫	Ranger station

0   .5   1
miles

Pretty Hollow Gap Trail–Palmer Creek Trail–Balsam Mountain Road–Spruce Mountain Trail–Polls Gap Trail–Rough Fork Trail.

Distance: 18.4 miles.

Elevation gain: 3,050 feet.

Brief trail description: This loop begins in Cataloochee, which is North Carolina's answer to Tennessee's Cades Cove. This huge mountain cove is the focal point for unusual mountain trails that, because of Cataloochee's remote location, are among the least-traveled routes in the Smokies.

How to get there: The entrance to Cataloochee is via old NC 284 (Cove Creek Road) immediately south of exit 20 on I-40. From the south or east, follow US 276 to Dellwood, North Carolina, turn right and continue on US 276. After 5.0 miles, turn left onto Cove Creek Road. This junction is 150 feet before the exit 20 ramp at the I-40 interchange. There is no sign marking Cove Creek Road. After 0.5 mile along Cove Creek Road, the pavement ends. After another 0.5 mile, a road to Suttontown branches left. The Cove Creek Road continues

right, climbing steeply 5.0 miles to the Park boundary at Cove Creek Gap. Cove Creek Road continues through the gap, descending 2.0 miles to Sal Patch Gap and the eastern terminus of the paved Cataloochee Road. To reach Cataloochee, turn left onto the new Cataloochee Road. After descending 3.0 miles, it crosses Cataloochee Creek to intersect the southern terminus of the old Cataloochee Road, a gravel track that leads to the Palmer house and then to the old NC 284. One mile beyond this intersection, the new Cataloochee Road passes the Cataloochee Campground with twenty-seven sites for vehicle camping. After the road passes a white church on the left, the parking lot for the Pretty Hollow Gap Trail will be on the right just before the road crosses Palmer Creek on a short bridge.

Recommended campsite: 42.

0.0—Cataloochee Road.

0.2—Horse camp.

0.8—Little Cataloochee Trail leads right 5.2 miles to old NC 284.

1.5—Indian Flats. Palmer Creek Trail leads left 3.3 miles to Balsam Mountain Road.

4.8—Balsam Mountain Road leads right 1.8 miles to the Spruce Mountain Trail.

6.6—Spruce Mountain Trail leads left 1.5 miles to the Polls Gap Trail.

7.6—Polls Gap Trail leads right 4.4 miles to the Rough Fork Trail at Polls Gap.

7.7—Path leads left 200 yards to backcountry campsite 42.

12.0—Rough Fork Trail leads left 6.4 miles to Cataloochee Road.

15.6—Caldwell Fork Trail leads right 6.3 miles to Cataloochee Road.

17.0—Backcountry campsite 40.

17.4—Woody Place.

18.4—Cataloochee Road.

This hike offers a little of everything. It starts with a comfortable walk along a cool mountain stream before ascending to one of the finest campsites in the Smokies. The second day brings a challenging walk along a forested ridge before returning to the Cataloochee Basin.

Cataloochee, in the southeast corner of the Park, is bounded by Mount Sterling Ridge, the Cataloochee Divide, White Oak Mountain, and Scottish Mountain. It is one of the least accessible major hiking areas in the Smokies. Within Cataloochee, several ridges divide the basin into a complex of coves, the largest of which is Big Cataloochee, a remarkably flat grassland extending along Cataloochee Creek and Rough Fork.

Before the Park was formed in 1934, Big Cataloochee was farmland that supported an isolated, agrarian community of nearly a thousand people. Of the two hundred or so buildings once scattered across this picturesque landscape, only a few remain—the Palmer, Caldwell, and Woody houses, the Will Messer barn, Beech Grove School, and Palmer Chapel. All of these are maintained by the Park Service and, except for

Big Cataloochee and Balsam Mountain from Cove Creek Gap. Courtesy of the Great Smoky Mountains National Park.

the Woody house, can be reached by automobile. Big Cataloochee's concentration of Appalachian architecture is second only to Cades Cove's.

Two other buildings, the John Jackson Hannah cabin and the Little Cataloochee Baptist Church, stand in Little Cataloochee, a subcove high under the lee of Mount Sterling and separated from Big Cataloochee by Noland Mountain. Though geographically distinct, blood and marriage join the two communities. Apple growing formed the economic base of the tiny hamlet of Ola, the provisional center of the farming settlements once clustered in Little Cataloochee.

The loop for this overnight hike begins at the trailhead to Pretty Hollow Gap Trail. The site of the earliest settlement in Big Cataloochee was clustered around the confluence of the Palmer and Cataloochee Creeks in a community later known as Nellie. The area was named for Nellie Palmer Wright, Turkey George Palmer's daughter, who had won first prize in a baby contest in 1901. As families moved into Cataloochee, a post office, church, and school were built in Nellie, making it the communal center of the cove.

The Pretty Hollow Gap Trail begins in Nellie a few yards above the confluence of the two streams. Directly across Palmer Creek from the trailhead is the schoolhouse. The first school on this site was built in 1895 and was originally called the Beech Grove School. It was later known variously as Shanty Branch School, Indian Creek School, and Big Cataloochee School. The name Shanty Branch was taken from the small stream that runs through the meadow on the far side of the schoolhouse. During the early part of the nineteenth century, this field was grazed by cattle belonging to Mitchell Davidson, a landowner from Jonathan Creek. Davidson's cattle were herded by a black slave named Old Smart who camped nearby in a shanty, thus giving rise to the name of the stream.

Sometime around the turn of the century, the citizens of Nellie decided that the schoolhouse was too small. The community petitioned the county commission for money to pay carpenters and buy paint. The commissioners claimed that they had no money and complained that Cataloochee did not pay enough taxes. That night, after the tables, books, and other items had been removed, the school burned, and Cataloochee got its new schoolhouse.

The Pretty Hollow Gap Trail follows Palmer Creek along a well-maintained jeep road to a large horse camp three hundred yards above the trailhead. At this point, the stream is wide and filled with many rapids and small falls. Cataloochee is a favorite destination for riders and their horses.

A half mile farther upstream, the Little Cataloochee trail exits to the left, leading up the side of Noland Mountain. Shortly above this juncture, the Pretty Hollow Gap Trail curls wide to the left, skirting a weedy clearing known as the John Mull Meadow, named for an early settler who operated a mill on Palmer Creek.

Originally the meadow extended several hundred yards along the stream to Indian Flats where Palmer Creek turns right near its confluence with Pretty Hollow Creek. Along here, the trail degenerates noticeably to a washed-out surface of loose glenstones. Following the stream, the trail turns left and proceeds one-quarter mile to an intersection with the Palmer Creek Trail near the mouth of Pretty Hollow Creek.

The Palmer Creek Trail begins on a footlog that crosses Pretty Hollow Creek near an old Indian camp known as Indian Flats. In 1875, Turkey George Palmer came to Indian Flats, where he found a small, cleared field with a disused fireplace and several scattered pieces of pottery. At the time of Turkey George's arrival, the stream running near the camp was known as Indian Creek.

Turkey George, one of the most colorful of Cataloochee's citizens, built a large house on Indian Flats about five hundred feet above Pretty Hollow Creek. It was a six-room, two-story frame building with two porches made of poplar. It bore two chimneys of handmade brick and was home to Turkey George until his death at a ripe old age.

When asked how he acquired his nickname, Turkey George gave the following account to Prof. Joseph Hall of Columbia University, who later recorded it in *Smoky Mountains Folks and Their Lore*. "I had a patch of land in corn. The wild turkeys was about to eat it up, so I built a pen to try to catch 'em. The pen was ten foot each way, and I covered over the top. Then I cut a ditch and run it into the pen and covered the ditch over with bark. I scattered corn in the ditch so as to draw the turkeys into the pen. Next mornin' they was nine big gobblers inside, an' one outside. I stopped up the hole an' got me a stick to kill 'em with. When I got in the pen, they riz up an' mighty nigh killed me instead; so I got out and fetched a hoe. When they stuck their heads betwixt the slats I knocked them with it. After that I built about three pens in the mountains an' caught two or three turkeys. That's why they call me 'Turkey George.' I reckon."

On leaving Indian Flats, the Palmer Creek Trail enters a narrow hollow separating Shanty Mountain from the southern end of Butt Mountain. The hollow, which channels the Palmer Creek, holds the finest northern hardwood forest in Cataloochee. The trail follows the stream, but only at a distance, climbing over a moderate grade along a well-maintained berm high on the slope of Butt Mountain.

A mile above Indian Flats, the trail crosses Lost Bottom Creek before Palmer Creek splits into Beech Creek and Falling Rock Creek. Here the trail crosses Beech Creek before following Falling Rock Creek to the crest of Balsam Mountain.

Falling Rock Creek is named for a freak accident that occurred in the Palmer Creek Hollow in 1922. Rev. Wilson Camel and a companion from Cosby, Tennessee, were spending a few days with Turkey George Palmer. Wilson and his friend were camping near the mouth of Lost Bottom Creek beside a large rock cliff. The weather was cool and the men built a fire large enough to last them through the night. Apparently, the heat from the fire loosened a large rock slab, which fell and crushed Reverend Camel in his sleep.

His companion, despite working all night, could not pry the rock off the preacher. At dawn, he waded down the creek (there was no trail at this date) to Turkey George's house. The teacher and some of the bigger boys from the nearby Beech Grove School assisted in freeing and carrying out the body. The homicidal slab is on the left side of Palmer Creek, about two hundred yards above the mouth of Lost Bottom Creek.

After crossing Beech Creek, the trail follows an old route once called the Trail Ridge Trail to the crest of the ridge. Here it turns for an easy route along the spine of Trail Ridge before terminating at the Balsam Mountain Road. At this juncture, the original Trail Ridge Trail turned right and descended along the course of the Balsam Mountain Road to Pin Oak Gap.

Turn left for an easy two-mile hike down Balsam Mountain Road to the Spruce Mountain Trail. The trailhead will be on your left. It is a short, one-mile, fairly steep hike to the junction with the Polls Gap Trail, which will intersect from the right. The final, unmaintained leg of the Spruce Mountain Trail leads left from this junction to the summit of Spruce Mountain. Even though several large trees lay fallen across the path and, in summer, this spur is heavily encumbered with overreaching blackberry briers, it is nonetheless a fine stretch of trail and is well worth the excursion. It is flat, firm, and soft underfoot. The fragile boreal humus footing is undisturbed by horses, and therefore free of the tiresome mud that accompanies much of the Polls Gap Trail.

Backcountry campsite 42, the Spruce Mountain Camp, is only two hundred yards down the Polls Gap Trail from the intersection with the Spruce Mountain Trail. This is an exquisitely unique little campsite nestled in a clearing carpeted with a thick turf of rich mountain grass. Well-spaced but huge spruce trees tower overhead. The camp, tucked between Chiltoes Mountain and Spruce Mountain, is one of the highest in the Smokies, and one of very few primitive, backcountry sites in the balsam zone. Thickets of rhododendron separate the tent sites, making the camp seem larger than it actually is. The water source is Bear Creek, a thin but dependable stream running gently through the camp's edge.

To resume the hike, return to Polls Gap Trail and turn left (south) for a one-mile ascent of Chiltoes Mountain. This ascent begins one of the most rugged yet rewarding trails in the Smokies. In the higher regions the firs grow in pure stands, crowding the trail in dense hedges where the tree boles are so thickset that one can see only two or three feet into the forest.

Although there are a few dead fir trees, the fir-killing fields found on the stateline divide and Mount Le Conte are missing on Balsam Mountain. The spruce, somewhat small along the trail, are most prevalent on the ridge points where spurs branch off the Balsam Mountain divide. Where the trail is fairly level, the balsam species thin, leaving open patches of blackberry brambles. Though clusters of fire cherry, beech, birch, and red maple occur regularly along the trail, the prevailing forest cover is a changing mix of spruce, fir, and blackberry brambles.

There is no real overlook from the ridge because the trail is hemmed in by a corridor of dense vegetation that only allows an occasional glimpse of the Cataloochee Basin. After about two miles the trail passes through Horse Creek Gap and then rolls over Cataloochee Balsam Mountain to begin a long descent down some very rough trail, which is badly eroded by horses. Just before it flattens out a bit for an easy half-mile finish to Polls Gap, the forest makes a transition to birch and beech.

Polls Gap, sometimes mistakenly called Pauls Gap, is a typical saddle gap hosting the junction of the Rough Fork, Polls Gap, and Hemphill Bald Trails. On one side of the gap, the Balsam Mountain Road passes on its way to the Heintooga Overlook. The gap was named for Aunt Polly Moody's cow, which died here while giving birth to a spring calf.

The route will take the hiker down Rough Fork Trail, which begins as a wide, abandoned railroad trace headed back down to Cataloochee. The stretch is an easy grade for the first two and a half miles through a second-growth poplar forest. The grade then increases as the trail descends a mile through virgin forest to a small gap along the spine of Big Fork Ridge, where the Caldwell Fork Trail enters from the right.

Rough Fork Trail drops through Hurricane Creek Ravine just before reaching Big Hemlock Backcountry Campsite (40), about a mile below the junction with Caldwell Fork Trail. The camp holds a labyrinth of rhododendron arranged among the big trees on the flat point between the two creeks. A path leads through an intricate passage to several tent sites, which are separated from one another like individual cells in a maze.

The trail exits on a footlog over Hurricane Creek and continues on for about a half mile to the Woody place, an attractive, two-story frame building built around a smaller log cabin. The cabin, situated in an open grassy clearing, was built in the late nineteenth century by Jonathan Woody, who first entered Cataloochee before the Civil War. During the first decade of the twentieth century, framed additions were added, which completely covered the original cabin. A spring house stands near the trail at the edge of the trimmed lawn.

The trail becomes a road as it leaves the Woody House and enters an impressive old-growth hemlock, beech, oak, ash, and poplar forest. A sparse understory graces the base of the trees except near the stream, where rhododendron abound. After about a mile, the trail terminates at a gate marking its intersection with a maintained road that runs for about a mile and a half back to the starting point. This is a wide-open trek through sweeping meadows, which frequently contain grazing deer. If there are two cars in your party, it might be a good idea to leave one at the gate to shorten the second day's hike. 🏃

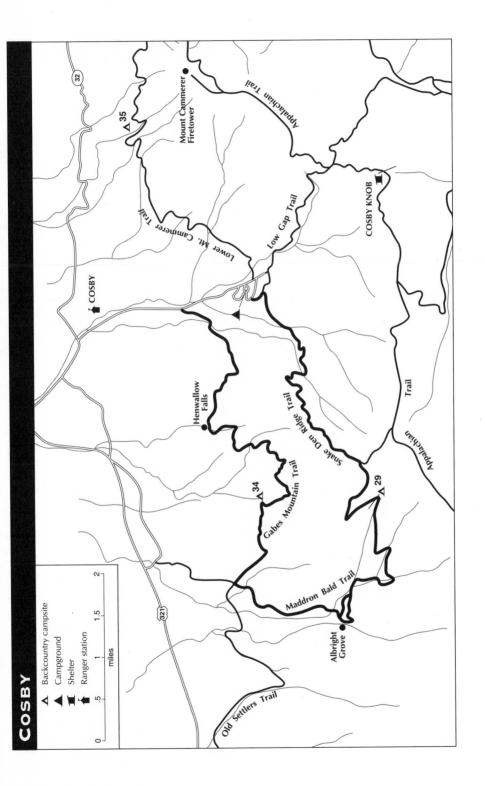

COSBY

- △ Backcountry campsite
- ▲ Campground
- ⛺ Shelter
- 🏠 Ranger station

miles

0   .5   1   1.5   2

32

△ 35

Mount Cammerer
Firetower

Appalachian Trail

Lower Mt. Cammerer Trail

Low Gap Trail

COSBY KNOB

⛺ COSBY

Henwallow
Falls

Snake Den Ridge Trail

Appalachian Trail

△ 34

Gabes Mountain Trail

△ 29

Maddron Bald Trail

Albright
Grove

321

Old Settlers Trail

Snake Den Ridge Trail–Maddron Bald Trail–Albright Grove Loop–Gabes Mountain Trail.

Distance: 17.7 miles round-trip.

Elevation gain: 4,100 feet.

Brief trail description: A visit to Albright Grove, one of the most magnificent stands of virgin forest remaining in the Park, is the high point on this loop.

How to get there: From Gatlinburg, drive south on US 321 to its intersection with TN 32 at the Cosby Post Office. Turn right onto TN 32 and drive 1.2 miles to Cosby Road leading right into the Park. Turn onto Cosby Road and drive 2.0 miles to the Cosby Campground registration station. From I-40, take exit 440 onto US 321. Follow US 321 south to its junction with TN 32. Follow the signs into the campground. The trailhead for the Snake Den Ridge Trail starts across from campsite B54.

Recommended campsite: 29.

0.0—Cosby Campground.

0.2—Connector leads left 0.4 mile to the Low Gap Trail.

0.7—Road turnaround.

4.6—Maddron Bald Trail leads right 6.1 miles to the Gabes Mountain Trail.

5.8—Maddron Bald.

6.1—Backcountry campsite 29.

8.6—Albright Grove Nature Trail loops left 0.7 mile.

9.3—Albright Grove Nature Trail returns to the Maddron Bald Trail.

11.0—Gabes Mountain Trail leads right 6.7 miles to Cosby Campground. Old Settlers Trail leads left 15.8 miles to Greenbrier Cove.

12.8—Backcountry campsite 34.

15.6—Henwallow Falls.

16.6—Road turnaround.

17.4—Trail splits. Right fork proceeds 0.3 mile to Cosby Campground and left fork proceeds 0.3 mile to Cosby Cove Road near the Cosby picnic grounds.

17.7—Cosby Cove Road.

This trail includes a visit to what is reportedly the finest stand of virgin forest remaining in the park. This overnight loop is in Cosby, in the northeast corner of the Park. Cosby, once known locally as the "Moonshine Capital of the World," is a small, circular basin tucked under the stateline divide. Cosby's slopes are furrowed with rocky, inaccessible hollows, once a curse to loggers, but a blessing to moonshiners.

The hike passes two significant points of interest.

The first, Albright Grove, is perhaps the finest stand of virgin cove hardwood forest in the Smokies. It is a remnant of the primeval forest that once blanketed much of North America. A forest so vast that it is said that, when Columbus landed in the West Indies, a squirrel could have traveled from Florida to Maine without ever having to touch the ground. The second landmark, Henwallow Falls, is an impressive cascade on the Gabes Mountain Trail.

The hike begins on the Snake Den Ridge Trail, which is, by any standard, an arduous climb. Every step is up. Nevertheless, it passes through one of the finest deciduous forests of North America. All the great trees of the Smokies are here—the poplar, beech, maple, hemlock, buckeye, Fraser magnolia, and locust. Higher up are a few pines and, higher still, the spruce, fir, cherry, and mountain ash.

The Snake Den Ridge Trail starts in Cosby Cove at the back of the Cosby Campground along a rehabilitated settlers' road. Four hundred yards up the road a connector branches left to the Low Gap Trail a half mile away. The road continues for another mile before terminating in a turnaround. A graded trail proceeds beyond the road, soon crossing Rock Creek on a footlog before entering the cathedral-like stillness of an old forest. Tree boles of enormous proportions stand on a boulder-strewn floor of rich, luxuriant undergrowth.

These old giants ascend without a limb for almost eighty feet before bursting out into an interlocking, shading canopy high over the trail. Here, the trail generally follows the course of Inadu Creek. The higher the trail ascends the valley, the deeper it penetrates to the heart of this dim, pristine wilderness.

Approximately one mile above the road turnaround, the trail leaves the Inadu Creek valley and ascends the side of Snake Den Ridge. The grade is steep and the climb strenuous. At the third switchback, the trail tops a ridge that offers a view into Cosby Cove.

Along the lower end of Snake Den Ridge, the forest begins a transition from the great hardwoods of the creek valley to the boreal stands of the balsam zone. The ridge, exposed and dry, is unable to support the huge cove specimens. As the trail follows the ascending ridge, the trees appear generally smaller, with some species disappearing altogether. Where conditions are particularly inhospitable—on the dry, eastern exposures—laurel and pines prevail. The trail, depending on its position on the ridge, alternates between deep woods and heath conditions.

A small heath bald along the ridge line affords the finest view on this trail: a good look at the main divide from Inadu Knob to Mount Cammerer. Higher up, at the edge of another exposure, there is a curious mix of pine, hemlock, fir, and spruce. This is odd because pines prefer hot, dry conditions, and the balsams cold and wet conditions.

Along here, the grade moderates noticeably. It proceeds deeper into the balsam zone and eventually intersects the Maddron Bald Trail ascending from the right. Less than one hundred yards beyond the junction is the disused Maddron Bald Backcountry Campsite, a small clearing with a spring below. This overnight loop, however, suggests a right turn on the Maddron Bald Trail.

From this direction the Maddron Bald Trail first descends gradually for about half a mile through a thinly mixed stand of boreal species, mostly spruce, fir, cherry, and ash, with clumps of rhododendron and patches of painted trillium providing the most noticeable undergrowth. The trail then opens into a slight, grassy swag that provides the entrance to the Maddron Bald.

Colloquially, Maddron Bald is called a "hell," an impassable, tangled mass of heath covering an extended area. This particular hell resides along the spine of a long ridge descending from Inadu Knob on the stateline divide. The enclosing heath thicket presses the trail to the apex of the narrow ridge where it remains for the next half mile. The wall of rhododendron and laurel is breached in only one or two places where sand myrtle–infested rock outcroppings jut out from the ridge. The best view is of Greenbrier Pinnacle across the valley to the west. The exit from Maddron Bald is marked by an extremely dense corridor of rhododendron and laurel.

After a mile and a half, the trail enters the Otter Creek Backcountry Campsite (29), a gently rolling site wedged between Otter Creek and a boulder field. This is a serviceable camping area with several gritty, almost gravelly, plots arranged terracelike along the grade. A steel cable is suspended across the camp for hanging packs out of the reach of foraging bears (but not out of reach of an industrious little red squirrel—so plan accordingly). The trail leaves the campsite and crosses Otter Creek, a major tributary of Indian Camp Creek.

After crossing the creek, the trail ascends for about three-quarters of a mile before entering a heath bald aligned along the spine of a minor ridge above the creek. Where the trail crosses over the ridge, a path turns right down the spine about twenty-five yards to a rocky outcropping that offers a fine view into the Indian Camp Creek valley. Greenbrier Pinnacle is the big mountain to the left with the high peaks of Mount Le Conte barely showing over the top edge of the ridge. The Old Black–Mount Guyot neighborhood of the stateline can be seen above the upper end of Pinnacle Lead. To the right is the high Maddron Bald ridge.

The trail leaves the heath bald and begins a series of five easy stream crossings of Indian Camp Creek and Copperhead Branch. Here it wanders through boulder fields strewn along the upper reaches of the Indian Camp Creek Watershed.

After close to four miles the upper end of the Albright Grove loop trail enters the Maddron Bald trail from the left. This loop leads through one of the most notable poplar-hemlock forests in the Smokies. Albright Grove is a virgin forest that was acquired from a logging and paper company before it had a chance to clear-cut it. It is probably the finest and most diversified stand of large, old-growth trees remaining in the Park. The Albright Grove Nature Trail passes the base of a yellow poplar thought to be the largest in the Smokies. The tree is 25 feet, 3 inches in circumference and stands 135 feet high.

In addition to the tulip trees, this narrow forest path also winds among exceptional examples of maples, Fraser magnolias, silverbells, and eastern Hemlocks. The thickness of their trunks, as opposed to their height, is the best evidence of their old age.

Albright Grove is named for Horace M. Albright, a Californian who was instrumental in shaping the framework of the National Park Service after it was formed by the Organic Act of 1916. Later, as director of the National Park Service, Albright adroitly garnered the necessary financial and political support to establish the Great Smoky Mountains National Park.

After completing a loop of seven-tenths of a mile, the Albright Grove Nature Trail rejoins the Maddron Bald Trail. From this point it is two miles to the junction with the Gabes Mountain Trail. About halfway down, the trail widens where an old settlers' road has been upgraded to a jeep road. The last mile of the Maddron Bald Trail is a comfortable walk along the jeep road.

Six miles down the mountain from its juncture with Snake Den Ridge Trail, the Maddron Bald Trail is joined by the Old Settlers Trail coming in from the left and the Gabes Mountain Trail heading out to the right. It is over six and one-half miles along the Gabes Mountain Trail back to the Cosby Campground. Allow three and one-half to four hours to cover this distance.

Generally, older trails in the Smokies follow the bed of a stream or the crest of a ridge. Only occasionally does the hiker have to proceed laterally to the streams and ridges, hopping from one watershed to another. The Gabes Mountain Trail, once known as the Messer Trail, is an exception; it crosses an alternating succession of streams and ridges between the Maddron Bald Trail and Cosby Cove.

Although this complex route makes it sound strenuous, the Gabes Mountain Trail

Henwallow Falls. Courtesy of the Great Smoky Mountains National Park.

is only moderately difficult. It sports an attractive waterfall and is graced by stands of virgin forest nestled around pretty streams. The trail immediately enters a forest marked with pockets of virgin hemlocks and poplars interspersed along the terrain of second-growth forests.

It was in this section that one of the authors almost had his heart stop a couple of years ago. We were hiking along on a pretty spring day, when we approached a tree which had fallen across the trail. There was enough room to swing under it, so he put both hands on the trunk and started under, only to come nose to nose with a large black snake that was sunning itself on the fallen tree.

To paraphrase Ross Perot, there was a large sucking sound as he inhaled all available oxygen and fell flat on his back. The snake, equally startled, darted down the trunk and shot into the underbrush. Black snakes are not poisonous, but check that tree trunk before you grab it nonetheless. We nearly always do now.

At close to two miles the trail enters the site of the Sugar Cove Backcountry Campsite (34). This attractive, boulder-strewn camping area is located on the western bank of Greenbrier Creek and offers several comfortable tent locations. The trail proceeds on a gently undulating course across streams, including Maddron, Buckeye, Greenbrier, and Gabes Creeks, before it traces the Lower Falling Branch downstream for about a quarter of a mile to Henwallow Falls. There is a short trail to the left which leads to the top of the falls. To reach the base of the falls and its cool pools of water, continue on for about a hundred yards to a second, larger trail that goes left and snakes down about two hundred yards to the base of the rock face.

Here the stream is shunted into a narrow aperture at the top of a sixty-foot cliff. Shooting through the opening, the water fans out quickly into a shimmering cascade that rolls down the bare face of the cliff wall. It is a particularly lovely spot on a sunny day.

According to a bit of tradition preserved by Carson Brewer in *Hiking in the Great Smokies,* the name "Henwallow" is the result of an act of spite on the part of one community toward another. Brewer records that a family living in a small, unnamed community near here had, one spring, ordered one hundred baby chicks from a hatchery. The family had intended to raise the chicks to egg-laying hens and sell their eggs. When the chickens became old enough for their gender to become obvious, the family counted ninety-five roosters and five pullets. Neighbors in another nearby, unnamed community thought this was rather funny, and they took to calling the first community "Roostertown." The Roostertownians responded by calling the first community "Henwallow." There was no real basis for the name Henwallow; the name was strictly an act of rhetorical revenge.

Today, neither the location of Henwallow nor Roostertown is known. Henwallow survives as a waterfall, and Roostertown exists only as the name of a road off US 321 just outside the Park.

After leaving Henwallow Falls, the trail winds over rocky terrain as it exits the Lower Falling Branch watershed of Henwallow Creek. Shortly, the trail encounters a clearing occupied by the trace of a turnaround, ostensibly the terminus of a disused farm road. This road runs back down to the Cosby Cove access road a short distance below the picnic grounds. The Messer Trail, predecessor to the present Gabes Mountain Trail, started at this turnaround and proceeded west out of Bearneck Cove.

The trail continues on uneventfully until, about twenty miles from where you began, it separates into a "Y," with each fork about a quarter of a mile long. The trail to the right leads to the western edge of the Cosby Campground, and the one to the left exits onto the Cosby Grove Road just below the picnic area. 🚶🚶

Pole Road Creek Trail

△ 54

△ 55

△ 56

△ 57

△ 61

Noland Creek Trail

△ 62

58 △

59 △

Deep Creek Trail

△ 60

Noland Divide Trail

Sunkota Ridge Trail

Loop Trail

Lonesome Pine Overlook

Indian Creek Falls

Indian Creek Trail

Creek Trail

Deep

△ Backcountry campsite

▲ Campground

🛖 Shelter

🏠 Ranger station

0   .5   1
miles

Deep Creek Trail–Pole Road Creek Trail–Noland Divide Trail.

Distance: 18.0 miles round-trip.

Elevation gain: 2,700 feet.

Brief trail description: This hike is an especially good one for those who would like to try a little trout fishing along the way on the first day. The location of the campsite makes it possible to catch dinner and fry it up over the campfire.

How to get there: To reach Deep Creek, drive south on the Newfound Gap Road out of the Park and into Cherokee, North Carolina. In Cherokee, turn right on US 19 and proceed 10.0 miles to Bryson City, North Carolina. Turn right at the old Swain County Courthouse onto Everett Street to cross the Tuckasegee River. Follow Everett Street two blocks, cross the railroad tracks and turn right onto Depot Street. Depot Street leads out of town to Deep Creek Road. The Deep Creek Campground is approximately 3.0 miles along Deep Creek Road.

Recommended campsite: 56.

0.0—Deep Creek Road.

0.2—Tom Branch Falls.

0.7—Indian Creek Trail leads right 0.1 mile to Indian Creek Falls.

1.7—Jenkins Place. Loop Trail leads right 0.7 mile to the Sunkota Ridge Trail and 1.2 miles to the Indian Creek Trail.

2.1—Road turnaround.

2.6—Backcountry campsite 60.

5.1—Backcountry campsite 59.

5.5—Backcountry campsite 58.

6.1—Backcountry campsite 57. Martins Gap Trail leads right 3.1 miles to the Indian Creek Trail.

6.6—Backcountry campsite 56.

6.8—Sassafras Ford. Pole Road Creek Trail leads left 3.3 miles to the Noland Divide Trail.

10.1—Upper Sassafras Gap. Noland Divide Trail leads left 7.9 miles to the Deep Creek Campground. Noland Creek Trail leads straight 8.9 miles to Lakeview Drive.

14.5—Lonesome Pine Overlook.

18.0—Deep Creek Campground.

The Deep Creek basin, bounded by the Thomas Divide on the east and the Noland Divide and Beaugard Ridge on the west affords some of the more rugged hiking terrain in the Smokies. This loop avoids the strenuous upper end of the Deep Creek Trail itself, which runs into the Newfound Gap Road just south of Newfound Gap. This loop begins in the more easily hiked bottom-lands around Deep Creek, approaching the Park boundary. The area is broken up by several short ridges, the largest of which is

Sunkota Ridge, an appendage of the Thomas Divide that separates Deep Creek from its main tributary, Indian Creek.

The Deep Creek lowland was one of the more heavily settled parts of the Smokies, especially along the wide bottoms flanking Deep and Indian Creeks. Like most inhabited Park areas, its woodlands were first selectively harvested by the pioneer settlers and then clear-cut by the loggers.

The Deep Creek Trail is a streamside course that forms the backbone of an extensive network of trails running north into the basin. The lower end is anchored in the Deep Creek Campground, a developed facility accommodating 108 campsites. For some reason, all eight backcountry campsites in the basin are clustered along the midsection of the Deep Creek Trail.

The rugged slopes immediately west of Deep Creek are accessible by the Pole Road Creek Trail, which climbs to Noland Divide, and by the Fork Ridge Trail, which leads to the Clingmans Dome Road on the stateline divide. The more hospitable region east of Deep Creek is laced with trails following the old traces left by settlers.

Deep Creek, although about the same depth as other major streams in the Park, was the deepest stream in the immediate area and accordingly received its name from early settlers. These pioneers lived and tended farms in the bottomlands along the stream. They left roads and farmsteads that today are marked by the trails and campsites scattered throughout the basin.

The Deep Creek Trail begins as an easy course over a jeep road along a nice stretch of the stream. About a quarter mile above the trailhead, a small cascade known as the Tom Branch Falls splatters down onto the rocks along the opposite shore of Deep Creek. A half mile beyond the falls, the road meets an old settlers' trace, now known as the Indian Creek Trail, entering from the right. We recommend a short excursion at this point onto Indian Creek Trail.

In the springtime, the lower portion of the Indian Creek Trail is host to a variety of wild flowers, including showy orchids, foamflower, crested dwarf iris, wild geranium, trillium, cutleaf toothwort, and others. Two hundred yards above the trailhead, a short path leads down to a large plunge pool fed by Indian Creek Falls, a foaming fifty-foot-long cascade.

After visiting this side trail, return to the Deep Creek Trail. The trail immediately passes the confluence of the Indian and Deep Creeks on a bridge and proceeds one mile to an abandoned farmstead, a wide, weedy clearing known as the Jenkins Place.

Here the road is intersected from the right by the Loop Trail, a lateral route leading a half mile to the Sunkota Ridge Trail and another half mile to the Indian Creek Trail. The road then runs out of the Jenkins Place before terminating in a dead end at a turnaround a half mile farther on.

Beyond the turnaround, the trail is a rough jeep track that leads to the Bryson Place, the most prominent placename on Deep Creek. The trail rolls up and down over several spurs off Sunkota Ridge through a forest of beech, basswood, maple, poplar, Fraser magnolia, and white pine. Between the spurs it follows closely by the stream, while at the top, each spur affords a view down the Deep Creek gorge.

Sixty years ago hikers would have been spared the effort of ascending and descending the spurs. Then, Deep Creek was visited primarily by people who hunted and fished. They followed an older route that crossed and recrossed the creek over a dozen times. They camped where they could ford the creek, and some of these former camps now hold backcountry campsites.

A half mile above the turnaround, the trail crosses a creek on a footlog and enters a small cove harboring the large Bumgardner Branch Backcountry Campsite (60). The Bumgardner Camp is noteworthy for the large grove of hemlocks shading the area. After exiting the Bumgardner Camp, the trail edges away from the creek and climbs a high finger ridge, several hundred feet above Deep Creek. From the ridge there is a magnificent view down into the gorge. The trail descends to cross another spur or two before passing through two more backcountry campsites, the McCracken Branch Camp (59) and the Nicks Nest Branch Camp (58).

The McCracken Camp lies along a bend in the trail in a clearing known originally as the McCracken Improvement. It has a nicer location with respect to the creek than its upstream counterpart, but is more exposed to the trail. The abundant white pines carpet both sites with a thin layer of cushioning needles.

Bryson Place, one mile and one spur crossing beyond the Nicks Nest Branch Camp, is the most well-known camp on Deep Creek. Bryson Place (57), an old camp established in the mid-nineteenth century, was a favorite campsite for three legendary Smoky Mountain figures—Samuel Hunnicutt, Mark Cathey, and Horace Kephart.

According to Hunnicutt, himself a turn-of-the century bear hunter, Bryson Place was "where the hunters hunting in that section usually camped." In Hunnicutt's time, Bryson Place held an assortment of shelters, mainly cabins and lean-tos, which were used by the numerous hunting and fishing expeditions. Its strategic location, just below the Sassafras Ford and near two trail junctions, afforded easy access to the many high ridges teeming with game around Deep Creek.

Sam Hunnicutt was a hunter with definite ideas on his sport: "I claim to be a perfect hunter and fisherman for game fish; I know the best kinds of hunting outfit to use, I know the best kind of gun to use for killing game and also the best dogs to use for hunting." Hunnicutt recorded many of his hunting and fishing adventures in an awkward narrative, *Twenty Years of Hunting and Fishing in the Great Smoky Mountains.* The book, even with its serious literary deficiencies, is, nevertheless, a fine collection of homespun yarns which familiarizes readers with the ridges, hollows, streams, gaps, camps, and nooks and crannies in and around Deep Creek.

Mark Cathey, like Hunnicutt a lifelong resident of the Deep Creek watershed, was also a fine hunter. He gained fame, however, as an outstanding dry-fly trout fisherman. Anglers came from all over to fish with him and to see him practice an unorthodox, but effective, technique of dancing the dry fly on the water's surface. In doing so, he departed from the more traditional method of casting and allowing the fly to float down the current.

Horace Kephart, the noted author of *Our Southern Highlanders,* also had a close association with Deep Creek during his years in the Smokies. Kephart, who had a penchant for establishing semipermanent camps and living in them for several months at a time made his last camp in Bryson Place.

Just prior to crossing the stream into Bryson Place, a faint manway leads left two hundred feet to a spot where a brass plaque is mounted on an old millstone. It reads:

On this spot
Horace Kephart, Dean of American Campers
and one of the principal founders of the
Great Smoky Mountains National Park
pitched his last permanent camp.
Erected May 30, 1931
by Horace Kephart Troop, Boy Scouts of America
Bryson City, North Carolina

Bryson Place once had a well-kept appearance, "like an English country park." Today the camp is an extensive area of hard-packed bare ground used principally as a horse camp. Whatever charm it may have had in Hunnicutt's day has vanished. The place is beyond worn, and the few broken-down tables and grates scattered about merely add to an air of despair.

In the middle of Bryson Place, near the small stream that runs down to Kephart's old camp, the Deep Creek Trail is intersected by the Martins Gap Trail descending from Sunkota Ridge. The route along the Deep Creek Trail edges out of Bryson Place along the lower, washed-out side of the camp.

Four hundred yards beyond Bryson Place, the trail enters a mile and a half stretch known as the Elliott Improvement. The improvement lies along Deep Creek, bordered below by Elliott Cove Branch and above by Nettle Creek. Sam Hunnicutt often distinguished between the Elliott Improvement and the upper Elliott Field. Hunnicutt's Elliott Improvement, which was occupied by a house, probably included the area between Elliott Cove Branch and the Pole Road Backcountry Campsite (55).

The area is unusually level and afforded Hunnicutt and his companions numerous excellent campsites. The lower end is now occupied by the Burnt Spruce Backcountry Campsite (56), a long narrow site that extends through a grove of white pine. Even without a creekside setting, it is one of the nicer camps along the trail. The camp is clean and far enough from the trail to be reasonably inconspicuous and is perhaps the best place to make camp for this particular loop hike.

Two hundred yards above this campsite is the Sassafras Ford where hunters crossed Deep Creek to pick up trails running up Pole Road Creek and the Left Fork of Deep Creek. The ford gave access to the Pole Road Creek Trail, a primary route for those trying to reach the higher ridges and remote recesses above Deep Creek. Today a footlog spans Sassafras Ford, making it unnecessary to wade Deep Creek.

The Pole Road Creek Trail begins at the far end of the footlog and turns up through the vale of a wide cove that flanks Deep Creek. Not more than 250 yards from the footlog, the trail skirts a flat spot that resembles an abandoned campsite. This spot was probably associated with a splash dam that stood a few yards away at the mouth of Pole Road Creek. The splash dam was used by loggers to accumulate water for floating poplar and basswood logs down Deep Creek to Bryson City.

A few yards beyond the campsite, the trail crosses the Pole Road Creek and turns left to trace the course of the creek, crossing it several times over the next two miles. Pole Road Creek receives its name from the skid trails built by loggers along the stream. They placed poles across the trails at short intervals so that logs could be skidded down the mountain on the poles rather than on the ground. This prevented the logs from catching on rocks or sinking into the soft ground.

Two miles up, the trail crosses a band of virgin forest. Most noticeable is a cool grove of large hemlocks towering over a sparse, muted understory of rhododendron. An association of beech, poplar, and Fraser magnolia on the drier contours adds a distinctive richness to this magnificent forest.

This trail's final mile begins with a climb along the edge of a shallow ravine, leading through a large thicket of rhododendron. Emerging from the thicket, the trail completes its final half mile through an open hardwood forest before terminating in the Upper Sassafras Gap on Noland Divide. Here two other trails meet the Pole Road Creek Trail. The Noland Creek Trail emerges from a dense rhododendron thicket to end in Upper Sassafras Gap opposite the Pole Road Creek Trail.

The Noland Divide Trail runs from the Deep Creek Campground, up and along Beaugard Ridge, then traces the ridgeline of Noland Divide to the Clingmans Dome Road. The route will take you left (south) back to the campground. A half mile from joining the Noland Divide Trail, the route passes through Lower Sassafras Gap. The trail will trace a dry ridge line covered with black locust, black cherry, and northern red oak. Large boles of fallen chestnuts lie scattered among the trees that replaced them. The chestnuts can be identified by the gray color of the aging wood and the vertical cracks along the trunks. At about two and one-half miles, the trail skirts the east side of Coburn Knob. About halfway around the knob, a small spring dribbles across the trail into a boggy patch on the other side. Right after passing the knob, there is a sharp switchback to the left, marking the transition from Noland Divide to Beaugard Ridge. A mile from the switchback, along the thinnest edge of Beaugard Ridge, a short twenty-five-yard-long manway leads from the right of the trail to a small promontory known as Lonesome Pine Overlook. This vantage point is suspended over Lands Creek basin, which lies between Beaugard Ridge and the southern end of Noland Divide. From here, there is a fine view down the curved spine of the rugged Beaugard Ridge, which descends to the edge of Bryson City. The town is clustered along the banks of the Tuckasegee River and bordered by a wide collar of green farm fields tucked tight against the first low ranges of the Nantahala National Forest.

The trail continues on a course for two miles, dropping down along the spurs of the ridge into the Juney Whank Branch drainage of the Deep Creek Basin. It descends onto a low ridge just before running the last mile or so through a level but damp stretch of hedgelike undergrowth and finishing with a small stream crossing prior to ending near the entrance to the Deep Creek Campground. 🏃

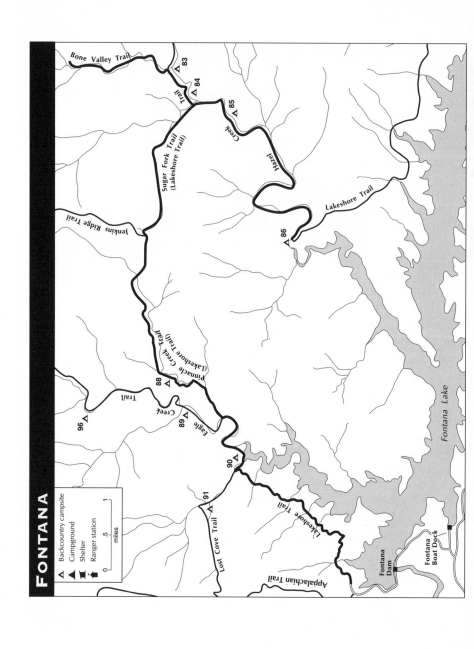

Hazel Creek Trail–Bone Valley–Sugar Fork Trail–Pinnacle Creek Trail–Eagle Creek–Lost Cove Trail–Lakeshore Trail.

Distance: 23.4 miles.

Elevation gain: 2,400 feet.

Brief trail description: A visually stunning boat ride across Fontana Lake to the mouth of Hazel Creek begins a hike into a once well-populated area of the Park, which is now isolated by the lake.

How to get there: There is no direct access to the Hazel Creek section. Hiking trails lead into the basin from the stateline divide and from the sections adjacent to either side. The most convenient and visually spectacular access is across Fontana Lake. A commercial shuttle to the Hazel Creek embay-ment is available from the Fontana Village Marina: (704) 498-2211. Fontana Village is located off the southwest corner of the Park along Route 28 and can be reached via Route 129 out of Maryville–Knoxville, Tennessee, and from Route 441 to Route 74 to Route 28 on the North Carolina side. Arrange-ments can be made to be picked up at Eagle Creek

rather than hiking out the last 5.2 miles to Fontana Dam.

Recommended campsite: 83.

0.0—Hazel Creek embayment at Proctor.

0.4—Backcountry campsite 86.

0.5—Lakeshore Trail leads right 21.3 miles to the Forney Creek Trail.

3.6—Backcountry campsite 85.

5.1—Backcountry campsite 84. Sugar Fork Trail leads left 2.4 miles to Pickens Gap.

5.8—Backcountry campsite 83. Bone Valley Trail leads left 1.8 miles to the Halls (Kress) Cabin.

7.6—Halls (Kress) Cabin.

9.4—Return to backcountry campsite 83.

10.1—Return to backcountry campsite 84 where the Sugar Fork Trail leads right 2.4 miles to the Pinnacle Creek Trail at Pickens Gap.

12.5—Pickens Gap. Pinnacle Creek Trail leads straight 4.1 miles to the Eagle Creek Trail. Jenkins Ridge Trail leads right 6.5 miles to the Appalachian Trail at Spence Field.

15.0—Backcountry campsite 88.

16.6—Eagle Creek Trail leads left 1.1 miles to the Lost Cove Trail and backcountry campsite 90.

17.7—Backcountry campsite 90. Lost Cove Trail leads left 3.2 miles to the Appalachian Trail at Sassafras Gap.

18.1—Lakeshore Trail leads left 5.3 miles to the Appalachian Trail near Fontana Dam.

23.4—Paved road begins. Appalachian Trail enters from the right.

This is a fine hike into a unique, but seldom visited, area of the Park. One can see firsthand the evidence of the evolution of development in the Park represented by the ruins of the hunting lodge in Bone Valley, the vestiges of the logging industry at Proctor, and Fontana Dam. The stateline divide between Thunderhead Mountain and Silers Bald forms the rim of the vast upper edge of the Hazel Creek basin. The basin is bounded on the west by the Jenkins Trail Ridge and its southern appendage, Horseshoe Ridge. The eastern boundary is defined by the long, crescent-shaped Welch Ridge, which curls down and underneath Horseshoe Ridge. From the headwall, hundreds of rills feed larger streams collecting in the tributaries that merge into Hazel Creek, the principal stream draining the watershed.

The Hazel Creek Trail begins about five hundred yards below Proctor at the makeshift boat landing along the head of the Hazel Creek embayment. Three hundred yards above the embayment, the trail passes the first of five campsites on Hazel Creek, the Proctor Backcountry Campsite (86). This rough-featured camp is large and its half-acre is partitioned by clusters of pines that make the camp appear smaller than it is. There are plenty of places along the water to enjoy the sights and sounds of the wide, easy-flowing Hazel Creek.

Sometime during the early part of the eighteenth century, Moses and Patience Rustin Proctor ventured up uninhabited Hazel Creek and built a cabin on a nondescript slope about one mile above the creek's confluence with the Little Tennessee River. Later, these pioneer settlers were joined by other families, eventually forming a community known as Proctor.

Calhoun House on Hazel Creek built in 1928. Courtesy of the Great Smoky Mountains National Park.

BEST OVERNIGHT HIKES

For many years Proctor was just a small village, a spot on the map in a remote corner of the Smoky Mountains. Sometime around 1909, the W. M. Ritter Lumber Company descended on Hazel Creek and turned Proctor into a logging industry boom town of over one thousand people. The newcomers graded mountainsides and built railroads, sawmills, drying kilns, milling ponds, pumping stations, roads, and splash dams.

Over the next fifteen years, the loggers removed 166 million board feet of timber, most of it virgin hardwood, leaving a scarred, burnt-over landscape of stumps and briers. After the loggers left, Proctor became a prime fishing destination, drawing enthusiasts to Hazel Creek's abundant trout.

Today Hazel Creek is quiet. The people are gone, and a fine second-growth forest has reclaimed the land. Nothing remains of the former boom town except for the road and the crumbling ruins of the abandoned kilns and pumping stations.

Two hundred yards beyond Proctor Camp, the Hazel Creek Trail meets the Lakeshore Trail approaching from the right. Here, the Hazel Creek Trail turns left and crosses the bridge over Hazel Creek. From this point to the Sugar Fork junction, the Hazel Creek Trail is part of the Lakeshore Trail.

On crossing the bridge, there is a white frame house down the road to the left. This is the Calhoun House, built by Granville Calhoun, the squire of Hazel Creek, in 1928, two years after the lumber company left Proctor. Before moving to Proctor, Calhoun lived five miles upstream at Medlin. Unlike his mountaineer neighbors, who lived in one-room log cabins, Calhoun maintained a five-room house for his wife, their three small children, and occasional boarders.

Calhoun built railroads for Ritter and was on a retainer with the Hazel Creek Mining Company and the Stikeleather Lumber Company, which later logged the upper end of Bone Valley. Largely because of his prominence in the community, Granville Calhoun was asked in 1918 to take the census along Hazel Creek.

The Calhoun House is the only structure along Hazel Creek to survive the Park movement. It is maintained as a ranger's outpost and storage facility for maintenance equipment. Along the road, three hundred yards below the house, is a cemetery occupying the slope that once harbored the first cabin raised by Moses and Patience Rustin Proctor. Moses Proctor and his wife are buried here.

We were eating breakfast at the picnic table (picnic tables are a real luxury on an extended camping trip) beside the Calhoun House one morning when a flock of at least thirty turkeys descended into the grass about thirty yards from us. Turkeys, the largest birds in the park, are extremely wary of people, and it was a real treat to see them this close. The flock milled around for a while, pecking in the grass, and then, one by one, they flew across the stream to the far bank and trotted into the woods. They were very methodical about crossing the creek and kept about a twenty-second interval between each take-off. When the last one had crossed, we finished our meal and set off upstream.

The Hazel Creek Trail runs upstream and follows the road along the creek for the next ten miles. This marriage of road and stream provides a comfortable hike along what may be the loveliest stream in the Smokies. The trail provides an easy grade when the backpacks are at their heaviest, so load up with good food for dinner.

The most visible reminder of the former logging operation is the shell of a large brick-drying kiln standing discretely near the back of a field to the left of the trail about a quarter mile above the Calhoun House. Nearby is the depression and face of a log-milling pond and two concrete pump sheds. Everywhere the human-made intrusions are slowly yielding to the agents of time, and the ruins seem haunted in some ways.

The trail continues upstream, proceeding around a giant curve known as the Horseshoe. It eventually passes the Sawdust Pile Backcountry Campsite (85), a long camp occupying an attractive setting over Hazel Creek. Before moving to Proctor, Granville Calhoun lived in the tiny hamlet of Medlin, five miles above Proctor where the Sugar Fork Branch conjoins Hazel Creek. Horace Kephart, once this country's foremost expert on camping and woodcraft, stayed in Medlin on his first night in the Smokies, boarding with Calhoun for a few days before moving to a permanent home on the Little Fork of the Sugar Fork.

Near the confluence of the Sugar Fork and Hazel Creek, the trail crosses a bridge over the main stream, then intersects the lower terminus of the Sugar Fork Trail just before turning right to cross a bridge over the smaller stream. (At this juncture, the Hazel Creek Trail ceases to be part of the Lakeshore Trail configuration. The Lakeshore Trail follows the Sugar Fork Trail.)

Medlin became a recognized placename in 1887 when the United States Postal Service established a post office at the junction. The postmaster was Marion Medlin, a preacher who also served as the local doctor and justice of the peace. The hamlet of Medlin stood in the triangle formed by the trail and the intersecting streams. This site is now occupied by the Sugar Fork Backcountry Campsite (84), one of the finest campsites in the Smokies. The camp is level and well shaded by tall, slender pines and commands an excellent position over the streams. While not large, the site is sufficiently roomy, and its features are fine, having none of the coarseness of a horse camp.

The crumbling remains of a building lie across the trail from the campsite on a bare hillside sloping to the edge of the Sugar Fork. Some scraps of metal and a ragged boxwood are the most obvious remnants of this former settlement.

A half mile above the Sugar Fork Camp is the destination of this leg of the hike: the Bone Valley Backcountry Campsite (83), a large, L-shaped camp sitting snugly in the corner formed by Bone Valley and Hazel Creeks. The camp is below the trail, separated by a small knoll once occupied by a church. The entire site is remarkably level and has several niches that make excellent campsites. A house belonging to Jack Coburn and his family once stood in the flat of the Bone Valley Camp. Coburn migrated to Hazel Creek from Michigan to work in the lumber camps. He was a friend of Horace Kephart's and was described by Kephart as being an outstanding pugilist.

After leaving the camp, the trail crosses a bridge over Bone Valley Creek and immediately intersects the Bone Valley Trail, which leads left two miles to the Hall (Kress) Cabin at the head of the valley. Sometime during the 1880s, a small heard of cattle that were grazing in an enclosed hollow between Thunderhead Mountain and Hazel Creek were caught in a sudden freezing snowstorm. Stranded in the snow and unable to reach shelter, the cattle perished. For many years afterward, bleached bones could be seen scattered along the floor of the hollow, which became known as Bone Valley.

Bone Valley was one of the last sections of the Smoky Mountains to be logged by the lumber companies. Before the loggers came, pioneer settlers cleared land on the wide bottoms along both sides of Bone Valley Creek for building cabins, growing orchards, and grazing cattle. The Bone Valley Trail is a rehabilitated settlement road that follows a streamside course through the valley. The trail is a quintessential country lane: quiet, unobtrusive, soft underfoot, and flanked alternately by the stream, woodlands, and overgrown clearings. The four wide, knee-deep stream crossings are among the easiest in the Smokies.

The rural innocence of the area is captured in a story told by Jim Gasque, whose uncle owned a lumber company and a hunting and fishing lodge on Hazel Creek. According to Gasque, one of his uncle's rangers was patrolling along Hazel Creek one morning when he found fresh footprints leading upstream into Bone Valley. The size of the prints indicated that two or three children, all barefoot, had headed into the valley. It was part of his job, the ranger decided, to go up and run them out. Some distance up Bone Valley Creek, at a bend in the stream, he stopped suddenly when he saw two small girls lying on the edge of the creek with their heads and shoulders just out of the water and their arms locked together.

The girls were lying across the mouth of a small inlet of backwater. In the pocket of backwater, a boy was half wading and half crawling, lunging now and then in an effort to catch something. The girls formed a barricade to prevent the prey from escaping into the main stream.

Eventually the boy was down on all fours, feeling around the bottom in the now muddied water. In an instant, a huge trout jumped into the air. Attempting to escape the pocket where it had been cut off, the trout made a long leap in the direction of the stream. It landed in the arms of the little girls. A second later, the boy joined them, trying frantically to hold the fish down in the shallow water. After a struggle, the boy emerged to the bank, his arms locked around the fish.

The ranger waded across the stream for a closer look at the children and their bucking, four-pound rainbow trout. The boy and the little girls rightfully were afraid that the ranger would take their fish. Instead, he told them to, "Take that fish and get down the creek. If you don't talk, that is one fish no one will ever know about."

The Bone Valley Trail ends in a buttonhook at the Hall (Kress) Cabin near the upper end of the valley. It was built around 1880 by Jesse Crayton Hall, who moved to Bone Valley with his wife, Mary Dills, and four small children in 1877. Later Hall built a herder's cabin on the stateline divide at Derrick Knob, a prominent landmark known for many years as Halls Cabin.

The Hall (Kress) Cabin has been substantially renovated since its original construction. It now stands on a block foundation and is adorned with framed, glass windows. Most conspicuous, however, is the absence of a fireplace and chimney.

At the edge of the woods, a few yards to the right of the cabin, a massive double chimney stands over a grid of concrete foundations, the ruins of the Kress hunting lodge. A few yards to the left of the cabin is a rudimentary trail leading one-quarter mile to the Hall Cemetery.

After exploring Bone Valley, retrace the route to the campsite and back down Hazel Creek until you reach the Sugar Fork Trail/Lakeshore Trail, which will intersect on the right. The Lakeshore Trail appropriates all or parts of the Hazel Creek, Sugar Fork, Pinnacle, Eagle Creek, and Lost Cove Trails to fashion a meandering course westward. The use of the name "Lakeshore Trail" is awkward, for it results both in the loss of old, familiar trail names and the disassociation of traditional names with long-standing trails.

Here the Lakeshore Trail leaves Hazel Creek to follow the Sugar Fork Trail two and one-half miles to Pickens Gap. The Hazel Creek terminus of the Sugar Fork Trail is not marked by a trail sign, but it can readily be identified by its close proximity to the Sugar Fork Backcountry Campsite (84).

Sometime prior to the turn of the century, the Adams mining company opened a copper mine along the Sugar Fork of Hazel Creek, far up under the lee of Thunderhead Mountain. A road was cut, leading from the mine along the Sugar Fork to Hazel Creek then down the creek to Proctor. Litigation over ownership soon closed the mine, and Horace Kephart got permission to occupy one of the mining company's abandoned cabins. To reach his new home, Kephart took the old mining road, a path that would later be known as the Sugar Fork Trail.

Kephart was notorious for moving from place to place, and his last camp was at Bryson Place on Deep Creek. In addition to his writing, he devoted himself to preserving the Smoky Mountain wilderness, and, as a result of his efforts along with those of other committed Park advocates, the heartland of the mountains was set aside as the Great Smoky Mountains National Park. He lived to see one of the highest peaks in the Smokies renamed Mount Kephart.

The Little Fork of the Sugar Fork of Hazel Creek, made famous by Kephart, can be reached from the former Sugar Fork Trail, now a renamed segment of the Lakeshore Trail. The trail begins at the Sugar Fork Backcountry Campsite (84) on the Hazel Creek Trail just above the confluence of the Sugar Fork and Hazel Creek. (The TVA quad maps identify this lower section of the Sugar Fork as the Haw Gap Branch.) From beginning to end, the trail adheres closely to the Sugar Fork, parting company only for the last few yards where it climbs into Pickens Gap. (As noted above, the Sugar Fork Trail is part of the Lakeshore Trail configuration.)

A half mile above the trailhead, two manways intersect the Sugar Fork Trail, one from each side. The one to the left leads one hundred yards to the Higdon Cemetery. The one to the right is the unmaintained Haw Gap Branch Trail, which leads to a network of trails that once served the large Bone Valley watershed.

A mile above this junction, the trail passes a clearing that indicates an old homesite. At the upper end of the clearing, an abandoned road trace leads to the old Everett Mines. The road, heavily overgrown in small trees and rhododendron, leads to two mineshafts on the east bank of the Little Fork. High on the west bank, across the stream from the second mineshaft, and on a level area at the foot of a deep draw is the site of Kephart's first home in the Smokies. It was a fourteen-foot-square log cabin with a tent attached to the side. Before Kephart, the cabin was occupied by a blacksmith working the mines. No trace of the cabin remains.

Shortly after Kephart left Little Fork, the lumber company moved in, leaving a desert of stumps and tangled debris to mark what had once been a pristine forest. Afterwards, Kephart wrote: "Not long ago I went to that same place again. It was wrecked, ruined, desecrated, turned into a thousand rubbish heaps, utterly vile and mean."

On passing the Little Fork, the trail skirts an old homesite and resumes its easy grade along the Sugar Fork. Four hundred yards from the end, the trail leaves the stream and begins a steep climb into Pickens Gap, where it meets the Pinnacle Creek Trail rising into the gap from the opposite side. To the right is the Jenkins Ridge Trail, running six miles to the stateline divide at Spence Field.

Upon reaching Pickens Gap, the highest point along the Lakeshore configuration, the Lakeshore Trail leaves immediately by way of the Pinnacle Trail, descending three and a one-half miles to cross Eagle Creek and connect with the Eagle Creek Trail. The Pinnacle Creek/Lakeshore Trail drops off the ridge following an old jeep track for the first half mile. It then narrows to a footpath as it winds above the Pinnacle Creek Gorge. The gorge is formed by the narrowing of Pinnacle Creek and the trail runs along the rim of the steep western side.

About two miles down, the trail runs into the Pinnacle Creek Backcountry Campsite (88), situated nicely in a small, partially level plat above the trail. Many campsites in the Smokies are former homesites or logging camps and have something of a domestic quality about them. The Pinnacle Camp is an exception. It is a backwoodsman's camp, a hidden, isolated niche in a recess beyond Eagle Creek.

A few miles beyond the campsite the trail begins the first of fifteen wet stream crossings. It is a good idea to put on an old pair of sneakers at this point and leave them on until this trail is behind you. The remaining trail is nearly always immersed in a thicket of large-limbed, sprawling rhododendron and several stands of huge pine trees, among the largest of their kind in the Park, flank the trail at irregular intervals. The trail, when not in the creek, is nicely cushioned with a mat of needles.

As the trail approaches the much larger Eagle Creek, it wanders briefly through a beech and pine forest. Until it was washed away in a spring flood in 1994, a slightly unsteady footlog spanned Eagle Creek and marked the lower terminus of the Pinnacle Creek Trail. Since the footlog is now missing, the trail begins in the creek, which is usually more than knee deep and sometimes quite swift.

At this juncture the Lakeshore Trail turns left off the Pinnacle Creek segment and traces a mile of the Eagle Creek Trail to the Lost Cove Backcountry Campsite (90). A few yards downstream from the camp, the Lost Cove Trail cuts in sharply to join the Eagle Creek Trail. Following the Eagle Creek Trail to this point, the Lakeshore Trail turns up the Lost Cove Trail and ascends the vale of a steep-sided, narrow hollow. A quarter mile up the hollow, the Lakeshore Trail leaves the Lost Cove Trail on a narrow path that appears as a sharp slash cut into the bank at the left side of the trail.

The next three and one-half miles are not easy. Generally, the trail crosses the Snakeden Ridge and then the Shuckstack Ridge. In doing so, it negotiates the hollows and spurs of the many finger ridges fanning out from the two major ridges. The grade along this section is severe, and the trail conditions are hard on the feet. One way to avoid this section is to arrange for the boat shuttle from the marina to pick you up at the Eagle Creek embayment at a prearranged time.

Near the foot of Shuckstack Ridge the trail yields to another section of disused road. The road rises through a small gap, then begins a long, winding descent to Fontana Dam, passing several abandoned automobiles along the way. Near the trail's end, a steel cable is stretched knee high across the road. A hundred yards beyond the cable, the Appalachian Trail descends to the road, marking the end of the Lakeshore Trail. The paved improvement continues another half mile to Fontana Dam. The walk across this towering dam is really impressive, especially if there is a water release and TVA is generating power.

Another good reason to walk out is to use the showers near the dam. Adjacent to the dam's Visitor Center, the Tennessee Valley Authority maintains shower facilities for hikers. Because this luxury is available to the hikers staying in a nearby shelter as they take on the twelve-hundred-mile Appalachian Trail, the shelter and its amenities have been informally dubbed the "Fontana Hilton." 🚶🚶

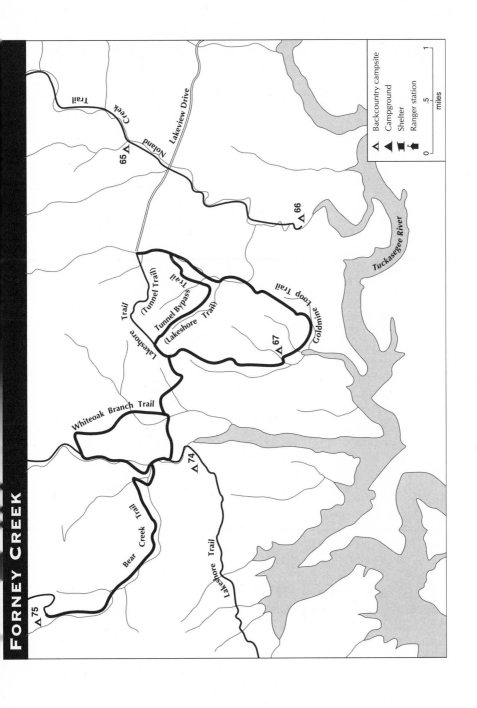

FORNEY CREEK

Backcountry campsite △
Campground ◀
Shelter ⛺
Ranger station

0 .5 1
miles

Tuckasegee River

Tunnel Trail
Tunnel Bypass
(Lakeshore Trail)
Lakeshore Trail
Goldmine Loop Trail
△ 67

△ 66

△ 65
Noland Creek Trail
Lakeview Drive

Whiteoak Branch Trail
△ 74
Bear Creek Trail
△ 75
Lakeshore Trail

Lakeshore Trail–Goldmine Loop Trail–Forney Creek Trail–Whiteoak Branch Trail–Lakeshore Trail.

Distance: 16.4 miles round-trip.

Elevation gain: 2,800 feet.

Brief trail description: The highlights of this loop include the excursion around Goldmine Loop, one of the more charming short trails in the Smokies, and a walk alongside the rugged Forney Creek. In addition, the embayments where Goldmine Creek and Forney Creek empty into Fontana Lake offer geographical features more reminiscent of Rocky Mountain meadows than Appalachian streams.

How to get there: From Gatlinburg, drive south on the Newfound Gap Road into Cherokee, North Carolina. In Cherokee, turn right on US 19 and proceed 10.0 miles to Bryson City, North Carolina. At the Swain County Courthouse, turn right onto Everett Street and cross the Tuckasegee River. Follow Everett Street through town (its name changes to Lakeview Drive) and continue 3.0

miles to the Park boundary. Lakeview Drive continues 5.0 miles into the Park to a parking area at the far end of a viaduct over Noland Creek. A path to Noland Creek Trail is at the upper end of the viaduct. Lakeview Drive terminates 1.0 mile beyond the viaduct at the mouth of a tunnel marking the head of the Lakeshore Trail.

Recommended campsite: 47.

0.0—Trailhead at Lakeview Drive.

0.4—Goldmine Loop Trail leads left 2.0 miles, looping back to the Lakeshore Trail.

1.3—Goldmine Branch embayment.

1.6—Manway leads right 0.2 mile to backcountry campsite 67.

2.4—Lakeshore Trail leads left 2.3 miles to the Forney Creek Trail.

3.6—Whiteoak Branch Trail leads right 1.8 miles to the Forney Creek Trail.

4.7—Forney Creek Trail leads left 0.2 mile to backcountry campsite 74 and right 0.3 mile to the Bear Creek Trail.

5.0—Bear Creek Trail leads left 2.8 miles to backcountry campsite 75 and 6.6 miles to High Rocks.

7.8—Backcountry campsite 75.

10.6—Return from backcountry campsite 75 to the Forney Creek Trail. Forney Creek Trail leads left 1.1 miles to the Whiteoak Branch Trail.

11.7—Whiteoak Branch Trail leads right 1.8 miles to the Lakeshore Trail.

13.5—Lakeshore Trail leads left.

14.7—Goldmine Loop Trail leads right.

14.8—Tunnel Trail leads left.

16.0—Goldmine Loop Trail leads right.

16.4—Lakeview Drive.

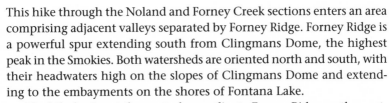

This hike through the Noland and Forney Creek sections enters an area comprising adjacent valleys separated by Forney Ridge. Forney Ridge is a powerful spur extending south from Clingmans Dome, the highest peak in the Smokies. Both watersheds are oriented north and south, with their headwaters high on the slopes of Clingmans Dome and extending to the embayments on the shores of Fontana Lake.

The hike begins at the crest of an outlier to Forney Ridge on the western edge of the Noland Creek watershed. The Forney Creek watershed lies immediately west of Noland Creek and is likewise drained by a primary stream that flows to Fontana Lake. The Norwood Lumber Company thoroughly logged much of the Forney Creek section, removing virtually all of the standing timber to within one mile of Clingmans Dome.

Then, in 1925, a fire fueled by the slash left by the logging operation scorched much of what remained. Afterward, when the Park was established, several miles of trail were graded through the Forney Creek section, following the railroad berms built by the lumber company. Many of the old trails have fallen into disuse, and today only the streamside course and a few lateral connectors are still maintained.

Between the Noland and Forney Creek embayments is the Goldmine Branch embayment, a small subsection that harbors the eastern terminus of the Lakeshore Trail. The Lakeshore Trail is a Park Service innovation, pieced together from disused roadways, old manways, newly graded trail, and sections borrowed from existing trails. It extends along the Park's southern boundary for nearly forty-five miles.

Current convention treats the entire course as though it were a single, unified trail. The name "Lakeshore Trail" is a misnomer. Along its forty-five-mile span, only a brief three-mile stretch affords anything more than a few fleeting glimpses of Fontana Lake. Nonetheless, the Lakeshore Trail begins in sight of a tunnel at the end of Lakeview Drive in an unobtrusive opening in the undergrowth.

From here it proceeds on a delightful two-mile bypass loop that follows along and over the nose of Tunnel Ridge, then back again to an intersection with the far end of the Tunnel Trail. (The Tunnel Trail is an alternative route about seven-tenths of a mile long that begins at the mouth of the tunnel. In the future, the Lakeshore Trail may begin at the tunnel, leaving the bypass as a vestigial connector.)

A half mile into the trail, where it crosses over the nose of Tunnel Ridge, there is a rather confusing intersection. Here the Lakeshore Trail turns right and proceeds over a mile and one-half to its rendezvous with the Tunnel Trail. The trail proceeding left is the destination, the Goldmine Loop Trail. It descends the ridge then loops back to meet the Lakeshore Trail a second time, two hundred yards below the junction of the Lakeshore and Tunnel Trails.

The Goldmine Loop Trail is, as its name implies, a loop. It begins with the Lakeshore Trail and ends with the Lakeshore Trail. It is short, only two miles long, and, as far as anyone knows, there was never a gold mine in this vicinity. Nevertheless, very few trails in the Smokies exhibit the variety of scenery as that found on this trail.

From its eastern terminus, the Goldmine Loop Trail climbs quickly up and over the nose of Tunnel Ridge, then runs the crest of a short spur through an association of oak, maple, and sassafras. At the end of the spur, the trail drops abruptly into the bottom of a deeply shaded little cove, passing, on the way down, through a belt of white pine. At the bottom is a deep recess shaded by stately hemlocks and thickets of rhododendron clustered along the banks of Tunnel Branch.

The trail follows the Tunnel Branch downstream three hundred yards to its confluence with the Goldmine Branch embayment and to an excellent vantage point for gazing down the slender embayment toward Fontana Lake. This is also a terrific spot to stop for lunch and enjoy the open vistas, a welcome relief from the foliage-shrouded trails that predominate in the Smokies.

Turning away from the embayment, the trail negotiates a short course up Goldmine Branch to a fork in the trail. The trail that forks to the right proceeds three hundred yards to a thinly wooded clearing occupied primarily by second-growth poplars mixed with slender hemlocks. A shallow, slow-moving stream flows silently along the edge of the clearing, and on its bank is a small, level plat designated as the Goldmine Branch Backcountry Campsite (67). The area around the camp appears to be an old farm field, and it makes a very hospitable camping spot. We once camped in this spot for a "gourmet" overnight stay. We carried in ribeye steaks for our entrée and charcoal briquettes so the steaks would have just the right flavor. We also brought a large bag of pistachio nuts to go with the wine during "happy hour." Unfortunately, we tossed the packs down while we explored the area and returned to find that a raccoon had eaten all but three of the nuts.

The left fork is the Goldmine Loop which, after leaving the intersection, stays tight against a rhododendron-infested bank while passing a sedgy field on its left. The weathered remains of an old house stand in the low flats at the upper end of the field. Beyond the field, the trail completes a deft switchback maneuver to begin a rather steep climb back to the Lakeshore Trail.

The Lakeshore Trail climbs slightly before beginning a one-mile descent to the flats flanking the lower Forney Creek drainage. The trail through the flats is a disused wagon road that once served a settlement in this lowland area. Another road, now known as the Whiteoak Branch Trail, exits right to an adjacent section of the former settlement. Piled stones, foundation ruins, and other remains lie in the overgrown fields flanking the Lakeshore Trail where it continues past the Whiteoak junction one mile to an intersection with the Forney Creek Trail.

At this point the Lakeshore Trail turns left and follows the Forney Creek Trail a half mile to the Lower Forney Creek Backcountry Campsite (74) on the Forney Creek embayment. The embayment is worth seeing, and it is a good idea to hide your gear off-trail and walk on down. The campsite itself is a worn spot with a commanding view of the embayment. The surface is covered with a tired mixture of thin, sooty dust and loose gravel. A picnic table and an outhouse toilet are welcome amenities.

Especially at dawn and dusk, the embayments along Fontana Lake are alive with deer that have come down to graze on the grass lining the banks of the lake. Forney

Creek, one of the faster-flowing streams on the North Carolina side of the Smokies, drains a wide basin bounded on the east by Forney Ridge and on the west by Welch Ridge. The Forney Creek valley was formerly inhabited by settlers who farmed the creek bottoms and grazed cattle on the high pastures, particularly Andrews Bald on Forney Ridge and Silers Bald at the head of Welch Ridge. From 1909 to 1920, the Norwood Lumber Company logged virtually all of the standing timber in the basin to within one mile of Clingmans Dome. The timber was hauled down the mountain on a railroad grade that traced a streamside course along Forney Creek. Five years after the lumber company departed, the watershed was devastated by fire fueled by the detritus left behind.

The lower two-thirds of the Forney Creek Trail follows the old railroad grade. The upper portion is an extension of the logging road with a concluding section of graded trail. The trail is indirectly accessible on its northern end from the Clingmans Dome parking area and on its southern end from the western tip of Lakeview Drive. Trails also approach Forney Creek from the outlying Hazel Creek and Noland Creek watersheds. The only direct access to the trail is by boat across Fontana Lake and up the Forney Creek embayment.

Within the first two miles, the Forney Creek Trail proceeds through three junctions. The first is at the edge of the Lower Forney Creek Camp, where the Lakeshore Trail starts west around Pilot Knob to begin the long journey to Hazel Creek. At the second junction, a half mile upstream, the Forney Creek Trail encounters the Lakeshore Trail again, this time as it proceeds east toward Noland Creek. The third junction occurs another half mile farther on, where the Bear Creek Trail crosses left over Forney Creek via a wide bridge. This loop leads back up the Bear Creek Trail to the campsite we recommend for this loop, backcountry campsite 75. It should be noted that many older Park maps do not show this campsite and, instead, show a now closed campsite on a section of the Lakeshore Trail as campsite 75.

The Bear Creek Trail is one of three accessing High Rocks, the most spectacular vantage point in this section of the Park. Two hundred feet west of the junction with the Forney Creek Trail, the Bear Creek Trail crosses a jeep bridge over Forney Creek and immediately skirts the upper edges of the former Bear Creek Backcountry Campsite. Although this site is now closed, it is still shown on many Park maps as backcountry campsite 73.

After leaving this closed site, the trail proceeds along an old railroad grade that leads across Bear Creek and up a narrow, steep-sided hollow, deeply shaded by towering hemlocks. Still following the railroad grade, the trail doubles back sharply and traces its way out of the hollow.

As the trail proceeds, it stays to the high side of the valley, above Bear Creek, with Pilot Ridge visible to the south. The ridge receives its name from the large number of copperheads that allegedly lived there. In the Smoky Mountain region, copperheads were often called pilot snakes because of a mistaken belief that they acted as pilots or guides that led rattlesnakes to and from their dens.

About two miles up, the trail enters an enclosed cove known as Poplar Flats. At the upper end of the cove the trail forks. The trail to the left is an abandoned manway that climbs up to Pilot Ridge and follows the crest to Cold Spring Gap on Welch

Ridge. The old manway is easy to track, but the going is often virtually blocked by undergrowth.

The Poplar Flats Backcountry Campsite (75) is in the upper end of Poplar Flats. This intimate, level campsite is in an attractive setting under a canopy of tall, slender poplars. In the morning, simply return to the Forney Creek Trail and turn left (north). One mile above the Bear Creek junction, the Whiteoak Branch Trail leaves right to circle back around to the Lakeshore Trail.

The Whiteoak Branch Trail is a two-mile connector between the Forney Creek Trail and the Lakeshore Trail. After a short, level stretch, it ascends a low ridge, then drops into a lowland that once harbored a small community.

Once, we surprised a group of three does just after we rounded the nose of this ridge. It was one of the few times we have been really close to deer and seen them before they saw us. They had all been grazing with their heads down, and we had frozen in place before they looked up. Deer have very poor eyesight when it comes to picking out shapes, but they have evolved to be keenly aware of any movement. We tried hard not to move, and they were not aware of us. The grass must have been particularly tasty because they continued grazing, even though they were extremely nervous and picked their heads up to look in our direction every few seconds. After about five minutes, we moved ever so slightly and they were away like three arrows shot from a bow.

Evidence of old homesites is noticeable at irregular intervals along the trail's course. The Whiteoak Branch Trail terminates in the Lakeshore Trail about one mile east of the Lakeshore Trail's junction with the Forney Creek Trail. From here, follow the Lakeshore Trail east (to the left), and the trail passes the first leg of the Goldmine Loop Trail on the right after a mile and a half. The next intersection will be with the Tunnel Bypass Trail on your right. This trail proceeds on a delightful, one-and-a-half-mile bypass loop that follows along and over the nose of Tunnel Ridge, then back again to an intersection with the far end of the Tunnel Trail. Then, simply exit through the tunnel or bypass it to the south.

The confusing little collection of trails around the tunnel was spawned by the dead-ended Lakeview Drive. In the 1940s the federal government promised to build a road, complete with a tunnel, through this section in return for land donated by North Carolina to the Park. Lakeview Drive is known colloquially as the "Road to Nowhere," and the broken promise is still a hot political topic in this part of western North Carolina.

If you hike around the tunnel, you will pass the other end of the Goldmine Loop Trail on the right about a half mile before you reach your car.

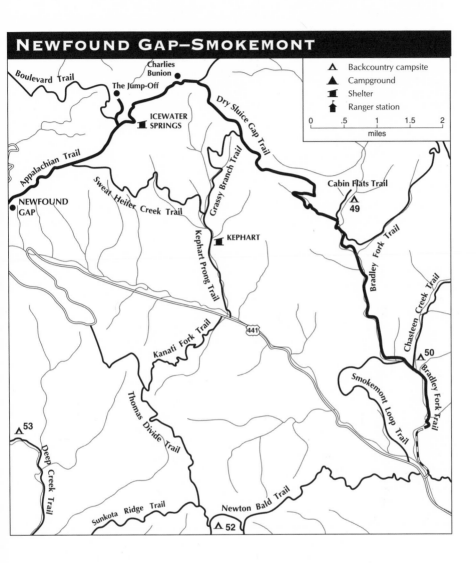

Backcountry campsite

Campground

Shelter

Ranger station

0 .5 1 1.5 2
miles

Boulevard Trail

Charlies Bunion

The Jump-Off

ICEWATER SPRINGS

Dry Sluice Gap Trail

Appalachian Trail

NEWFOUND GAP

Sweat Heifer Creek Trail

Grassy Branch Trail

Cabin Flats Trail

△ 49

Bradley Fork Trail

Kephart Prong Trail

KEPHART

441

Kanati Fork Trail

Chasteen Creek Trail

△ 50

Bradley Fork Trail

Smokemont Loop Trail

△ 53

Thomas Divide Trail

Deep Creek Trail

Sunkota Ridge Trail

Newton Bald Trail

△ 52

Appalachian Trail from Newfound Gap–Dry Sluice Gap Trail–Cabin Flats Trail–Bradley Fork Trail.

Distance: 14.2 miles.

Elevation gain: 1,100 feet.

Brief trail description: This, the only "downhill" hike, is best saved for a clear day when the spectacular views from the Jump-Off and Charlies Bunion allow hikers to enjoy these unique spots fully.

How to get there: The trailhead for this hike is at the Newfound Gap parking lot. The parking lot is 12.9 miles from the Sugarland Visitor Center, near Gatlinburg, Tennessee, and a little over 15 miles from the Oconaluftee Visitor Center, near Cherokee, North Carolina. The trailhead is located in the northeast corner of the parking lot near the restrooms. To do this as a two-car hike, first drop a car at the Smokemont Trailhead for Bradley Fork Trail. As a one-car hike, it is fairly easy to hitch a ride from Smokemont up to Newfound Gap to pick up your car.

Recommended campsite: 49.

0.0—Newfound Gap.

1.7 Sweat Heifer Trail leads right 3.7 miles to the Kephart Prong Shelter.

2.8—The Boulevard Trail leads left 5.4 miles to Mount Le Conte. Manway to the Jump-Off lies 200 feet above the junction of the Boulevard and the Appalachian Trails.

3.1—Icewater Spring Shelter.

4.1—Charlies Bunion.

4.5—Dry Sluice Gap Trail leads right 8.4 miles to Smokemont.

5.8—Grassy Branch Trail leads right 2.5 miles to the Kephart Prong Trails.

8.7—Cabin Flats Trail leads left 0.6 mile to backcountry campsite 49 and right 0.3 mile to the Bradley Fork Trail.

9.3—Backcountry campsite 49.

9.9—Return to the Dry Sluice Gap Trail intersection.

10.2—Bradley Fork Trail leads straight 4.0 miles to Smokemont.

12.5—Smokemont Loop Trail leads right 3.9 miles to the Smokemont Campground.

13.0—Chasteen Creek Trail leads left 4.1 miles to the Hughes Ridge Trail.

14.2—Smokemont Campground.

This trail begins with spectacular and breathtaking panoramic views, includes a picture-perfect campsite, and ends with an idyllic hike along a rushing mountain stream. It is predominantly a downhill hike, beginning in Newfound Gap at 5,000 feet above sea level and ending at Smokemont Campground after having dropped 2,700 feet of elevation. The first leg of the hike, the Appalachian Trail to the Jump-Off is the only up-hill portion of the hike and is one of the few trails in the Smokies that offers spectacular views at both its beginning and end. Both the Jump-Off and Charlies Bunion are the real visual payoffs for this loop.

Charlies Bunion is a unique rocky outcropping, scoured of all its topsoil by fire and erosion. The Bunion sits astride the Appalachian Trail, high above a winding gorge. The Jump-Off, a rugged point on the other side of the gorge, gives a view across to the Bunion and a look straight down several hundred feet into the gorge itself.

Another important plus for this hike is the fact that most of the elevation is gained through horsepower rather than leg power and carrying a full backpack downhill beats uphill every time. The trailhead is to the left of the paved walkway down to the restrooms on the northeast corner of the parking lot. A walkway below the parking area provides sweeping views into the deep gulf separating the stateline divide from Thomas Ridge. Beyond the gulf, layers upon layers of mountains roll in a blue haze deep into North Carolina.

Before the advent of the Park, Newfound Gap was an insignificant swag in the Smokies crest, not even distinguished by a trail. The gap was eventually widened to make room for a transmountain highway, now known as the Newfound Gap Road. When the highway was completed, a rockwork platform was built into the slope on the north side of the gap and served as a dais when President Franklin D. Roosevelt officially dedicated the Great Smoky Mountains National Park in 1940.

The trail to the Jump-Off and Charlies Bunion begins at the rockworks and follows the Appalachian Trail northeast out of Newfound Gap. The grade is moderate, and the trail a bit rocky in places. There are no views along this initial stretch except where the forest cover opens momentarily for glimpses of the distant North Carolina ranges. A half mile above Newfound Gap, the rocky course grades into a broad fairway that extends along the stateline divide to the foot of Mount Kephart. Though the path is a bit wet in spots, the hiking here is like strolling through a great wooded park. The trail is marked by stands of large spruce and birch with little undergrowth. Thick mountain grass frequently carpets the sides of the trail, and, at several intervals, short side paths lead up to the ridge line, offering views of the North Carolina mountains.

Except for a brief climb or two, the path is disturbed only by the Sweat Heifer Trail intersecting from the right. Otherwise, it continues on its leisurely pace, arriving after another mile at the base of Mount Kephart and a junction marking the head of the Boulevard Trail. Here, the trail to the Jump-Off goes left, following the Boulevard Trail and the trail to Charlies Bunion goes right following the Appalachian Trail.

The trail to the Jump-Off is a well-maintained manway that exits right from the Boulevard Trail one hundred feet above its junction with the Appalachian Trail. It leads over the summit of Mount Kephart and out to the Jump-Off, covering a distance of slightly more than one-half mile. Prior to reaching the Jump-Off, the manway levels briefly for a very fine view of the east end of Mount Le Conte and the Boulevard, the crooked, razor-thin ridge that connects Mount Le Conte with the main Smoky divide.

From this perspective, all of the peaks of Mount Le Conte are visible. To the right of Le Conte is the conspicuous pale green swatch on Brushy Mountain, a heath bald that graces the long northern flank of Mount Le Conte. Mount Kephart, like many peaks in the Smokies, offers no view from its highest point. The Jump-Off serves as the vantage point from Mount Kephart. The east edge of the Jump-Off is a vertical cliff that drops a thousand feet into a vast gulf. In the Smokies, only the Chimneys and Greenbrier Pinnacle offer a comparable spine-tingling view into an abyss.

The steep south wall of the gulf is formed by the stateline divide meandering to an indeterminate point in the east, with Laurel Top, Mount Chapman, and Mount Guyot arrayed prominently along its crest. The far end of the gulf is defined by Greenbrier Pinnacle, the massive lead that ends abruptly over Greenbrier Cove. Behind the Pinnacle is the distinctive anvil-shaped English Mountain.

To the left, rising from the bottom of the gulf is Horseshoe Mountain, aptly named for its own distinct shape. The grotesque rock promontory to the right, immediately across the gorge, is Charlies Bunion. The naming of Charlies Bunion is a curious piece of Smoky Mountain lore. In 1929, a resident of Oconaluftee named Charlie Conner was retained to lead a party trying to locate and name known topographical features. The group included Horace Kephart, the noted author of *Our Southern Highlanders*. While crossing a small knoll, Conner's feet began hurting. He complained to his companions about his hurting feet, mentioning something about a bunion. Later, while standing at the Jump-Off and surveying the steep declivities of the Tennessee slopes, Conner pointed to an unnamed hump on the

Charlies Bunion. Courtesy of the Great Smoky Mountains National Park.

stateline divide and said "That's just about like my bunion," or words to that effect.

"Then we'll call it Charlies Bunion," replied Kephart, and the name stuck.

The trail to Charlies Bunion begins back at the intersection of the Boulevard and the Appalachian Trail. At this juncture, the Appalachian Trail leaves the ridge and proceeds around the North Carolina side of Mount Kephart, descending shortly to the Icewater Spring Shelter, a stone structure situated nicely on a broad, rolling knoll just below the trail. This setting is among the finest of all the shelter sites in the Park. The area is open, level, and fairly carpeted in thick grass.

For several years the shelter included two permanent residents, Priscilla and Elvis, a pair of skunks who made their home under the first tier of bunks and emerged every evening around dinner time to share a good fire and a hearty meal with the campers.

Beyond Icewater Spring, the trail descends slowly for about two miles along a rough course that leads to the foot of the barren Charlies Bunion. The Bunion is an association of stark cliffs, ramparts, and jagged ridges scorched black in a 1925 forest fire that swept up and over the mountain from the North Carolina slope. Prior to the fire, the Bunion area was densely matted with a spongy carpet. The dense stands of fir left few visible traces of the rock underneath. Four years later, a thunderstorm plowed into the mountain, sending a flood of rainwater onto the burned-over Bunion. When the deluge hit, the once-burnt, water-soaked earth lost its grip and slid into the steep ravine below, carrying away all the vegetation and leaving nothing but the sheer rock behind. The tree trunks swept away in the flood are still visible, piled like kindling in the narrow, naked defiles a thousand feet below.

On Labor Day, 1951, a second flood visited the Bunion, this time washing out the thin vegetation that had managed to regain a tenuous hold on the scoured rock. Today the Bunion is still largely devoid of vegetation, dotted with a few clumps of sand myrtle, and remains, as noted mountaineer Harvey Broome once suggested, "a barren monument to man's carelessness with fire and nature's excess with water."

Standing on top of Charlies Bunion and looking into the dizzying depths of the ravine, one notices immediately a naked, razor-thin spine extending like a buttress between the base of the Bunion and a small knob. The sides of the spine are hideously steep, falling sharply away to the ravine below. Altogether, it is an unparalleled example of the underlying bedrock of the eastern Smokies.

The geography observable from Charlies Bunion is essentially the same as that from the Jump-Off; however, the perspective is different. Charlies Bunion lacks the long panorama down the stateline divide and the sense of altitude of the Jump-Off. On the other hand, the Bunion is a more hospitable resting place. Keep an eye out for the hawks which frequently ride the updrafts in the gorge looking for prey.

The Bunion provides ample spots to sit and soak up the spectacular scenery and, for the lucky hiker, some sunshine. It is a great place for a leisurely picnic lunch before beginning the hike to Cabin Flats.

After leaving Charlies Bunion, follow the stateline divide east along a sharply serrated ridge known as the Sawteeth. The westernmost of the Sawteeth's jagged peaks are separated by Dry Sluice Gap, a V-shaped notch that harbors the upper terminus of the Dry Sluice Gap Trail. At the upper end of the gap, the trail leaves the Appalachian Trail and begins a climb up the adjacent Richland Mountain.

The name Dry Sluice Gap comes from a spring that bubbles out of the mountain on the Tennessee side. Shortly, it sinks beneath the surface and flows unseen for several hundred yards. The fact that the stream flows in a subsurface channel is the reason for the name "Dry Sluice."

After departing Dry Sluice Gap, the trail negotiates steep slate ledges while curling along the flank of Richland Mountain to a position directly opposite the stateline divide. Across the ravine, the distinctive, jagged edges of the Sawteeth outline in bold relief the rugged contours of the divide. Left of the Sawteeth is the bare protrusion of Charlies Bunion, shadowed by Mount Kephart to the west.

Farther along, the trail curls back to the right, bringing into view the long southern flank of Mount Kephart. In cooler seasons, when the trees are free of leaves, the green roof of the Icewater Spring Shelter is clearly visible on the brown, tree-clad slope of Mount Kephart.

The same 1925 fire that scorched Charlies Bunion incinerated the intermediate ravines lying between the Stateline Divide and Smokemont, leaving only the blackened boles of once-virgin trees. The burned-over area recovered to a grassland, which was invaded by thin stands of mountain-ash, pin cherry, and yellow birch. Today, where the Dry Sluice Gap Trail passes through this recovered area, the forest remains sparse, affording fine views into the Oconaluftee valley.

About one mile below Dry Sluice Gap, the trail rolls off the ridgeline and into a slight depression that harbors the upper terminus of the Grassy Branch Trail. This intersection is surrounded by several Norway spruce trees, an exotic species planted here by the Champion Fibre Company after the fire in 1925. At this juncture, the Dry Sluice Gap Trail begins descending steeply along the eastern flank of the Richland Mountain ridge, grading easily from a red spruce association to one primarily of eastern hemlock, and then finally to an undisturbed hardwood forest of oak, poplar, silverbell, and basswood. For whatever reason, this enclave was spared both the logger's ax and the fire that scorched much of the immediate mountainside.

Upon entering the hardwood forest, the trail approaches the Tennessee Branch of Bradley Fork, where it becomes rockier, and often wet and muddy. It maintains a streamside course for three-quarters of a mile before terminating at the midpoint of a connector known provisionally as the Cabin Flats Trail. The Cabin Flats Backcountry Campsite (49) is about a half mile along this trail to the left, and the Bradley Fork Trail is a similar distance downstream.

The Cabin Flats Trail is a continuation of the jeep road along Bradley Fork and runs along the jeep track, following the curvature of Bradley Fork into an enclosed cove. A half mile up the cove, the trail drops to the Cabin Flats Backcountry Campsite (49), a remarkably flat acre sitting on the bank of Bradley Fork. The Cabin Flats Camp is among the most attractive and accommodating in the Smokies. Each campsite is situated on the bank of the stream, with ample space and a level plat. The trail enters the camp from the upstream end, then proceeds to its terminus at the last camp downstream where a pole is provided for hanging packs from the reach of inquisitive (and perpetually hungry) bears.

Begin the hike out by rejoining Bradley Fork Trail at the turnaround. From here, it is an extremely pleasant four-mile walk to Smokemont. A half mile down, the trail crosses the stream near the confluence of Bradley Fork and the cascading Taywa Creek. It later makes a double crossing of Bradley Fork, with the two crossings separated by an island in the middle of the stream.

At close to two and one-half miles the Smokemont Loop Trail will exit to the right, and three miles from the turnaround the trail passes the lower terminus of the Chasteen Creek Trail just before it crosses a feeder stream. The forest throughout this interval is a typical second-growth association of poplars and oaks, and, except for an occasional homesite clearing, the trail is uniformly pleasant in appearance and comfortable in its grade.

The lower part of the Bradley Fork Trail is a wide, even jeep track that rises easily along the banks of the boulder-studded Bradley Fork of the Oconaluftee River. This entire trail is particularly well suited for leisurely strolls in the woods, especially when the trees are adorned with their fall colors.

The trail ends at the upper end of Smokemont, where the Bradley Fork swerves gently to circumvent the large campground. The campground itself is a large facility designed for large camper vehicles, and the smell of fried bacon or barbecued chicken will often greet you long before the trailhead comes into view.

These smells often attract bears as well. A ranger friend once recalled a scene of a confrontation between a large bear and a large party of picnickers. When he arrived, he found a grandmother with a large frying pan in her hand stationed at one end of a picnic table and a bear standing, front paws on the table, at the other end. In the middle, its future in doubt, was a large birthday cake she had baked for her grandson. Every time the bear would reach for the cake, she would swat his paw with the pan.

Luckily, the ranger was able to save the cake and salvage the party by hustling the bear out of the picnic grounds. 🏃

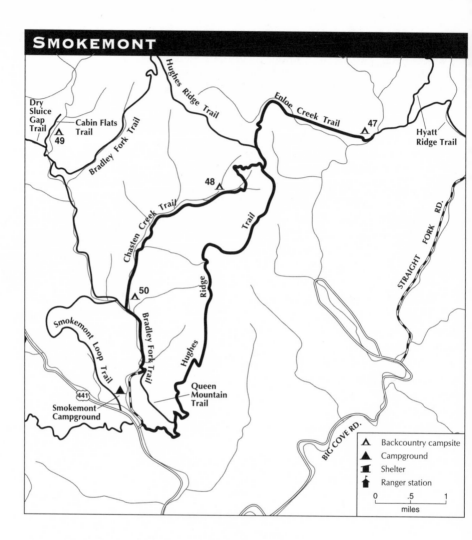

SMOKEMONT

Dry
Sluice
Gap
Trail

Cabin Flats
Trail

Hughes Ridge Trail

Enloe Creek Trail

Hyatt
Ridge Trail

A 47

A 49

Bradley Fork Trail

Chasten Creek Trail

A 48

Trail

Hughes Ridge Trail

A 50

Bradley Fork Trail

Smokemont Loop Trail

STRAIGHT FORK RD.

Queen
Mountain
Trail

441

Smokemont
Campground

BIG COVE RD.

A   Backcountry campsite
▲   Campground
◗   Shelter
♦   Ranger station

0   .5   1
miles

Bradley Fork Trail–Chasteen Creek Trail–Enloe Creek Trail–Hughes Ridge Trail.

Distance: 18.6 miles round-trip.

Elevation gain: 2,800 feet.

Brief trail description: One of the more picturesque campsites in the Smokies highlights this hike into a rugged wilderness area.

How to get there: From Newfound Gap, drive south 13.8 miles to the Smokemont Campground or, from the Oconaluftee Visitor Center, drive 3.2 miles north. The Bradley Fork Trail begins at the gate blocking the jeep road at the upper end of the campground.

Recommended campsite: 47.

0.0—Smokemont Campground.

1.2—Chasteen Creek Trail leads right 4.1 miles to the Hughes Ridge Trail.

1.3—Backcountry campsite 50.

3.6—Backcountry campsite 48.

5.3—Hughes Ridge Trail leads left 0.4 mile to the Enloe Creek Trail.

5.7—Enloe Creek Trail leads right 2.6 miles to backcountry campsite 47.

8.3—Backcountry campsite 47.

10.9—Return to the Hughes Ridge Trail. Hughes Ridge Trail leads left 7.2 miles to Smokemont.

11.3—Chasteen Creek Trail leads right to the Bradley Fork Trail.

17.1—Queen Mountain Trail leads right to the Bradley Fork Trail.

18.1—Bridge over Oconaluftee River, 0.5 mile below the Smokemont Campground.

This is a short but rugged hike into a spectacular wilderness area of the Park. It begins as an easy walk along the lower part of the Bradley Fork Trail, a wide, even jeep track that rises gradually along the banks of the boulder-studded Bradley Fork of the Oconaluftee River. The Cherokees gave the name Oconaluftee, meaning "by the river," to a collection of small Indian villages along the banks of the river flowing south from Newfound Gap through Smokemont to Tuckasegee. White settlers later named the river itself Oconaluftee.

The Oconaluftee River traces the Oconaluftee Fault, a fracture in the bedrock of the mountains. The basin that holds the Oconaluftee River is blocked at the upper end by a sweeping headwall that extends along the stateline divide from Newfound Gap through Mount Kephart to Pecks Corner. Hughes Ridge bounds the east side of the basin, and the Thomas Divide defines the western edge. Richland Mountain divides the basin and separates the Oconaluftee River from its main tributary, the Bradley Fork.

In the latter part of the nineteenth century, white settlers made the Oconaluftee valley the most heavily settled region in the Smokies. In 1831, the North Carolina General Assembly authorized the Oconaluftee Turnpike Company to build a wagon road up the Oconaluftee River and over the stateline divide at Indian Gap. The turnpike was completed in 1839 and, for several years afterward, operated as a toll road.

This unimproved toll road was used by logging companies before being upgraded in the 1930s to become the highway that crosses Newfound Gap. Smokemont, at the junction of the Bradley Fork and the Oconaluftee River, is a focal point for hiking trails in this section. From this point, trails lead onto Hughes Ridge and into the Bradley Fork drainage.

The Cherokees who inhabit the Qualla Reservation, bordering this corner of the Park, are members of the Eastern Band of the Cherokee Nation, a remnant of the Cherokee tribe members who were moved west on the infamous Trail of Tears. By the time white settlers had begun moving into the Smokies in the early nineteenth century, the Cherokees had become a "progressive" nation and had made many cultural changes in order to adjust to the influx of white European culture. For the most part, the Cherokees lived on farms and dressed like the white settlers. They built schools, published a newspaper, and established a republican form of government complete with a constitution and legislature. Their leaders were well educated and were capable of representing themselves in treaty negotiations before Congress.

In 1828 gold was discovered on Cherokee lands, prompting the state of Georgia to annex Cherokee lands by renouncing all treaties and revoking the Cherokees' personal legal rights. In 1835, by the so-called Treaty of New Echota, the Cherokees ceded to the government all of their territories east of the Mississippi. The Cherokees petitioned to Congress, but it was to no avail. In the winter of 1838, sixteen thousand Indians were ousted from their ancestral homeland and forced to walk all the way to Oklahoma. Several thousand perished due to starvation and cold.

About one thousand Cherokees hid in the high, remote recesses of the Smokies where federal troops were unable to hunt them down. Many starved or froze to death, but those that survived became the nucleus of the Eastern Band of the Cherokees. This remnant was later given money to buy what is now the Qualla Reservation, and Qualla residents obtained legal property rights to their lands. As the trail descends into the Enloe Creek campsite, it will be easy to see how the Cherokee were able to elude the government's soldiers in wilderness areas such as these.

The Bradley Fork Trail traces a broad, even roadbed alongside a picturesque mountain stream. The trail quickly enters a typical second-growth hardwood forest of poplar and oak, intermittently broken by an old homesite clearing. A mile above Smokemont, the trail crosses a feeder stream, then intersects the lower terminus of the Chasteen Creek Trail. The Chasteen Creek Backcountry Campsite (50) is two hundred yards to the right of this intersection. Follow the Chasteen Creek

Trail as it climbs above Smokemont to the crest of Hughes Ridge. Because the Chasteen Creek watershed was completely logged from the valley floor to the top of the ridge, the forest cover along the trail is second growth, mostly oak and maple.

The Chasteen Creek Trail begins as a jeep track, and, for most of its climb up Hughes Ridge, the trail traces the course of the stream, crossing it once on a bridge about four hundred yards above the camp. Along its lower stretch the trail is fairly level, but soon after crossing the bridge, the grade begins to steepen. The four miles of Chasteen Creek Trail are by far the most arduous of the hike.

About two and one-half miles above its lower terminus, the trail enters a deep draw, channeling several rills that feed into the main stream. Here the trail turns right, crossing the smaller streams and entering a large, terraced gradient harboring the Upper Chasteen Creek Backcountry Campsite (48). The camp, wide at its upper end, narrows as it slopes to the confluence of Chasteen Creek and one of the feeder streams. It is bare, except for several tall, ramrod-straight poplars and a few scattered clutches of small hemlocks.

About a half mile above the camp, the jeep track ends in a turnaround and a horse trail takes over. Not far above the turnaround, the trail cuts left, crossing several headwaters of Chasteen Creek as it works across the face of Hughes Ridge. It switches back right to complete a final, half-mile ascent to its terminus on a flat swag along Hughes Ridge. The upper end of the Enloe Creek Trail is a half mile up the ridge to the left along the Hughes Ridge Trail.

The Enloe Creek Trail enters the Hughes Ridge Trail from the right. The trail drops off the ridge line and immediately makes the transition to wilderness. This route is a gateway to the Raven Fork Basin, one of the most isolated and inaccessible wilderness areas in the Smoky Mountains. Very few trails approach the Raven Fork, and only one, the Enloe Creek Trail, actually penetrates to the bottom of the watershed. But even the Enloe Creek Trail is only a lateral connector, and it passes quickly across the lower aperture of the basin, linking Hughes Ridge with Hyatt Ridge, a short spur that separates the Raven Fork from its main tributary, the Straight Fork.

The trail quickly drops off the ridge and winds its way down to Enloe Creek. At first, the creek is a distant roar to the left of a trail that is often encumbered by stinging nettle, blackberry, wild hydrangea, fly-poison, touch-me-not, crimson bee balm, and black-eyed Susan. Several yards below the trail, Enloe Creek takes a much wilder course, plunging over three or four waterfalls and sliding down long, rocky shoals. There are several spots along this stretch for surveying the Enloe Creek valley and the balsam-clad upper reaches of Hughes Ridge.

About a mile from Hughes Ridge, the trail crosses Enloe Creek on a footlog and continues along the stream. For the two or three hundred yards approaching the crossing, the trail conditions are poor, often just a muddy quagmire. Weedy growth still encumbers the trail, except where densely shading spruce have claimed turf near the trail's edge.

After the crossing, the trail marks an easy course along the slope above Enloe Creek. Conditions here are wet and lush, and the virgin forest of maple, beech, cherry, oak, basswood, hickory, and hemlock towers above the valley floor.

The roar of Raven Fork greets hikers just before the trail drops down into the Enloe

Creek Backcountry Campsite. In our opinion, this is easily the most attractive setting for a campsite in the Smokies. It sits on a low bluff directly over the stream. The Raven Fork, confined by craggy cliffs and overhanging ledges, flows around great boulders thirty to forty feet in diameter and plunges down cascades into swirling eddies and deep pools.

Behind the camp, the mountain rises in a massive wall of jumbled boulders matted with a variety of dense, lush shrub species that thrive in the crevices between the rocks. The campsite is the only flat spot in this uncompromising terrain. It is a small, rigidly defined plot only large enough to accommodate two or three tents. There is a bear pole along the edge of the site for storing foodstuffs out of reach. A steel frame bridge, running from the side of the campsite high above and across Raven Fork, adds to the site's charm, while providing access to a deep pool that is perfect for a cool dip after a hot summer day's hike.

A couple of years ago we were packing up for the hike out when we noticed that our $140 charcoal water filter was missing. We broke both our packs completely down and methodically scoured the campsite, only to come up empty-handed. We remembered leaving it on a stump the night before, safely stowed in its little nylon sack. After searching for over an hour, we crossed over the bridge to get some drinking water that would have to be laced with our emergency supply of iodine pills. When we reached the far streambank, we found the filter, still in its sack, lying in some weeds. Only the drawstring on the sack was missing. Obviously, a raccoon had visited our site during the night and taken a liking to the colorful item. We learned a valuable lesson about securing every single item before turning in for the night.

For the return trip, trace the route back up the Enloe Creek Trail to the Hughes Ridge Trail. Go left at the junction and follow Hughes Ridge back to Smokemont. The first three miles are generally flat and follow the ridge line. Along the way the trail skirts the edge of Becks Bald before descending gradually through several switchbacks. Here the trail alternates between dry, barren patches rimmed with pines and laurel, dense, dark tunnels of rhododendron, and pockets of lush, leafy undergrowth shaded by cove hardwoods. It passes through the Qualla Indian Reservation just before it is joined, at about the four-mile mark, by the Queen Mountain Trail, which descends about one and a half miles to the right to the Bradley Fork Trail just above Smokemont. This hike continues on the Hughes Ridge Trail to Smokemont, just below the campground. 🏃

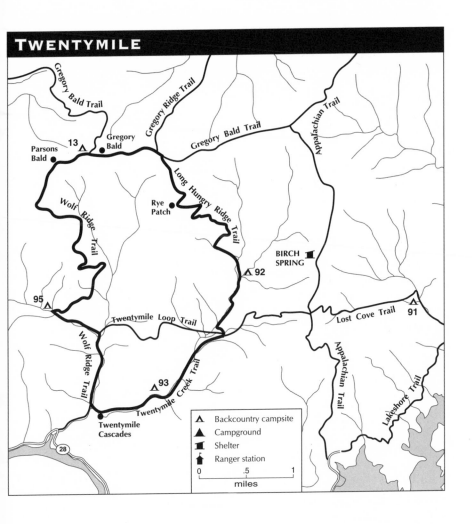

Parsons Bald
Gregory Bald Trail
Gregory Ridge Trail
Gregory Bald Trail
13
Gregory Bald
Appalachian Trail
Wolf Ridge Trail
Rye Patch
Long Hungry Ridge Trail
BIRCH SPRING
92
95
Twentymile Loop Trail
Lost Cove Trail
91
Wolf Ridge Trail
93
Twentymile Creek Trail
Appalachian Trail
Lakeshore Trail
Twentymile Cascades
28

Backcountry campsite
Campground
Shelter
Ranger station

0   .5   1
miles

Twentymile Trail–Long Hungry Ridge–Gregory Bald Trail–Wolf Ridge Trail–Twentymile Trail.

Distance: 15.8 miles round-trip.

Elevation gain: 3,200 feet.

Brief trail description: This hike, highlighted by two unique and interesting Smoky Mountain balds, features a trek through a remote and rugged section of the Park.

How to get there: From Knoxville, take Route 129 out of Knoxville through Maryville to Route 28 (toward Fontana Dam) to the parking lot at the Twentymile Ranger Station. From Cherokee, take Route 19 to Route 74 (Bryson City) to Route 28 past Fontana Village to the parking lot at the Twenty-mile Ranger Station. The Twentymile Creek section can be reached by driving the Foothills Parkway to its terminus at US 129, turning left, and driving on US 129 and NC 28 18.0 miles to the Twentymile ranger station or, from Fontana Dam, by driving 5.2 miles west along NC 28.

Recommended campsite: 13.

0.0—Twentymile ranger station.

0.5—Wolf Ridge Trail leads left 6.4 miles to the Gregory Bald Trail at Sheep Pen Gap.

0.6—Twentymile Cascades.

1.8—Backcountry campsite 93.

3.1—Proctor Field Gap. Long Hungry Ridge Trail leads left 4.6 miles to the Gregory Bald Trail at Rich Gap. Twentymile Loop Trail leads left 2.9 miles to the Wolf Ridge Trail.

4.2—Backcountry campsite 92.

6.8—Rye Patch.

7.7—Rich Gap. Gregory Bald Trail leads left 135 yards to its intersection with the Gregory Ridge Trail and 0.8 mile to Gregory Bald.

8.5—Gregory Bald.

8.9—Sheep Pen Gap. Backcountry campsite 13. Wolf Ridge Trail leads left 0.8 mile to Parsons Bald.

9.7—Parsons Bald.

13.3—At switchback, path leads right 100 yards to backcountry campsite 95.

14.2—Twentymile Loop Trail leads left.

15.3—Twentymile Creek Trail leads right to ranger station.

15.8—Twentymile ranger station.

Although the best time to take this loop is in early June when the wild azaleas are in bloom on Gregory Bald, both Gregory Bald and Parsons Bald make this a premier overnight hike anytime of the year. These trails are in a remote area of the Park and provide an uncrowded wilderness hike. We have never run into another hiker at Parsons Bald or on the Long Hungry Ridge Trail.

The Twentymile watershed is in the southwest corner of the Park. It is bounded on its north and east sides by the southern curvature of the stateline divide and on the west by Shuckstack Mountain and Twentymile Ridge. Between these boundaries, the watershed is subdivided by the Wolf Ridge and Long Hungry Ridge, which form the drainages for its two primary streams, Moore Spring Branch and Twentymile Creek.

Hiking in the Twentymile section is rewarding even though it can be rigorous. Geography requires a long car ride to gain access to the trailhead, and the trails on the first day of the hike are fairly steep. The Wolf Ridge and Long Hungry Ridge Trails follow a north–south axis running from the lower reaches of the valleys to the crest of the main divide at Parsons Bald and Gregory Bald respectively.

The trailhead is located at the end of the road leading past the Ranger Station to the parking lot. According to one tradition, Twentymile Creek gets its name from the fact that the distance from the mouth of Hazel Creek to the mouth of Twentymile Creek is twenty miles. The Twentymile Trail gets its name from the stream it follows through the glen defined by the adjoining Long Hungry and Twentymile Ridges.

The trail is a jeep road that extends from the Twentymile ranger station to the Appalachian Trail at Sassafras gap. For this hike you will cover only the first three miles of the road to the junction with Long Hungry Ridge Trail. The grade going in this direction is much less steep than if the hike were reversed and you had to come up the Wolf Den Ridge Trail.

After leaving the ranger's station, the trail ascends along Twentymile Creek, crossing a bridge over the Moore Spring Branch about a half mile up. At the crossing, the Wolf Ridge Trail exits to the left, climbing to the stateline divide at Parsons Bald. Two hundred yards above this junction, the Twentymile Trail passes a path leading down to the creek and the Twentymile Cascades. The cascades are a series of short, uneven ledges that preface a deep pool at the base of the lowest falls.

In several places, Twentymile Creek is a maelstrom of crashing water, roaring against solid boulders as it plunges down steep gorges. The trail, however, avoids the ruggedness of the stream by staying to an old roadbed, a veritable walk in the country. Even when it crosses the stream, it does so on a sturdy bridge, high and safe above the water.

Two miles above the ranger station, at the fourth bridge crossing, the trail passes Twentymile Creek Backcountry Campsite (93). From the camp the trail climbs to Proctor Field Gap to meet the Twentymile Loop and the Long Hungry Ridge Trails. Both trails exit left of the Twentymile Creek Trail, with the Twentymile Loop Trail farthest to the left. Take the Long Hungry Ridge Trail.

Sometime in the early twentieth century, a party of bear hunters reportedly were stranded on a ridge above Twentymile Creek, unable to cross the stream swollen by heavy rains. During the long wait, they nearly starved to death; hence the name, Long Hungry Ridge. Whether accurate or not, the story underscores the fact that Smoky Mountain streams can unexpectedly become raging torrents, impossible to ford.

The Long Hungry Ridge Trail begins east of its namesake where the Twentymile Creek Trail enters Proctor Field Gap, a rough settlement clearing that still bears remnants of stone fences and foundations. The trail proceeds north out of Proctor Field Gap along an abandoned railroad grade built in the 1920s by the Kitchen Lumber Company. After an easy crossing of Proctor Branch, the trail turns left and picks a streamside course along Twentymile Creek.

A mile above Proctor Field Gap, the trail crosses two feeder streams that drain a small basin known as Upper Flats. On crossing the second stream, Greer Branch, the trail leaves the railroad trace and enters the Upper Flats Backcountry Campsite (92). This camp is a loose grouping of four or five level plats fitted in the angle between Greer Branch and Twentymile Creek. A thin copse of tulip poplar, maple, and cherry trees shades the flats and defines the perimeters of the individual sites.

One hundred yards above the camp, the Long Hungry Ridge Trail crosses Twentymile Creek and begins climbing alongside Rye Patch Branch. From this point, the trail will gain about 2,100 feet of elevation in about three miles. A half mile above the Upper Flats Camp, the trail turns sharp right, crosses Rye Patch Branch, and enters a long, winding ascent of the eastern flank of Long Hungry Ridge. In places the grade is fairly steep.

The climb to the ridgeline terminates in the Rye Patch, an expanse of gently rolling land nestled in a slight swag in Long Hungry Ridge. The Rye Patch once served variously as farmland and grazing range, and bore the appearance of a grassy

Cades Cove from Gregory Bald. Courtesy of the Great Smoky Mountains National Park.

bald. Now, Rye Patch is neither clearing nor woodland. Instead, its thick turf is thinly shaded by a sparse stand of mixed hardwoods, giving it the pleasant appearance of a park.

After reaching the Rye Patch, the trail turns immediately right and follows the spine of Long Hungry Ridge one mile, terminating in the stateline divide at the east end of Rich Gap. Between the Rye Patch and Rich Gap, the grade is fairly moderate, affording a leisurely stroll through beech forests.

At Rich Gap, the Long Hungry Ridge Trail intersects the Gregory Bald Trail. Two hundred and fifty yards to the right, at the west end of Rich Gap, the Gregory Bald Trail intersects the Gregory Ridge Trail leading up from Cades Cove. Years ago, when cattle still roamed the high ridges of the Smoky Mountains, Rich Gap was a clearing occupied by something called a "gant" lot, a Smoky Mountain term that is missing from the dictionary.

A gant lot, according to these mountains' foremost chronicler, Horace Kephart, was "a fenced enclosure into which cattle are driven after cutting them out from those of other owners. So called because the mountain cattle run wild, feeding only on grass and browse, and 'they couldn't travel well to market when filled up on green stuff; so they're penned up to get *gant* and nimble.'"

Gregory Bald, famous for harboring the most brilliant display of flame azaleas anywhere in the Smokies, is three-quarters of a mile west of Rich Gap. Harvey Broome, a noted observer of the Smoky Mountains, described the azaleas on Gregory as being "of diverse hues, running from pure white through all the pinks, yellows, salmons, and flames, to deep saturated reds," and "ranged in such delightfully unstudied stands around the edge it seemed as though it had all been done by design." The azaleas blossom around the first of June and reach their peak about the middle of the month.

Gregory Bald is a ten-acre, dome-shaped clearing that sits astride the Tennessee–North Carolina border. It was once prized by cattle farmers as a rich upland grazing range. Members of several notable Cades Cove families herded at Gregory Bald. Russell Gregory was the first to build a cabin on the bald. His cabin was a cylindrically shaped, stone structure with large windows he called "portholes." In the evenings, Gregory would poke his rifle, nicknamed "Old Long Tom," through one of the "portholes" and shoot deer that approached to lick salt set out for the cattle.

There is long-standing speculation that Gregory is a natural bald. William Davenport, an early explorer who charted the main crest of the Smokies in the 1820s, recorded seeing two "bald spots" in this vicinity of the Smokies. The proximity of the bald spots suggests that Davenport was referring to Gregory and the nearby Parsons Bald.

In Davenport's day, Gregory Bald was much larger, the view less obstructed, and the atmosphere more clear than it is now. Accounts by early visitors suggest that as many as five states could be seen from the bald. Then, all of Cades Cove was visible as well as Happy Valley and the windings of the Little Tennessee River. The views from Gregory Bald today are inhibited by encroaching forests that block the line of vision to the south and west. Nevertheless, Gregory Bald still affords the finest vantage point in the Smokies for an all-encompassing view of the Cades Cove basin.

The trail exits the far (west) end of Gregory Bald and descends a few hundred yards before entering Sheep Pen Gap, host to the Sheep Pen Gap Backcountry Campsite (13). One of the finest campsites in the Park, it is the only primitive camp on the stateline divide. The gap is a flat, shallow swag situated about midway between Gregory and Parsons Balds. The half-acre clearing is covered with thick, rich mountain grass and shaded by sporadically placed clusters of serviceberry and oak trees.

There are several excellent tent sites, each well drained and cushioned by the thick grass. Two bear lockers are provided to safeguard food, and water is available from a big spring, albeit nearly three hundred yards down the Gregory Bald Trail.

The spring has two outlets. The first is about seventy-five feet off the trail to the downhill side and marked by a wet-weather creek that crosses the trail. The second, smaller outlet is just off the trail about fifty feet farther on. At dawn and dusk, deer wander out of the adjacent forest to graze on the abundant mountain grass. We have never camped in this spot without having at least three or four deer approach to within fifty feet of us.

The Wolf Ridge Trail runs southwest out of Sheep Pen Gap for about a mile through a grovelike canopy of birch trees with an understory of white snakeroot before it turns almost due south at Parsons Bald. Like all the other balds in the Smokies, this one has its own unique character. With its tall grass and occasional stunted tree, it seems more like an idyllic homesite than a pasture.

According to mountain lore, Parsons Bald was occasionally the site of religious camp meetings, where a parson would hold forth with colorful services. The name "Parsons Bald" supposedly was suggested by the camp meetings, and the nearby Bible Creek and Testament Branch give credence to this explanation for the bald's name. Another theory holds that the bald was named for Joshua Parson, an influential settler who lived near the confluence of Abrams Creek and the Little Tennessee River. His name is also associated with Parsons Branch Road and Parsons Turnpike.

At the center of Parsons Bald is a small patch of thick turf, the remnant of a grassy expanse that once served as a grazing site for cattle. Since the arrival of the Park, the forest has been slowly encroaching on the grassland and has reduced the bald to a small plot. Before trees blocked the views, Parsons Bald offered spectacular overlooks into the lake district. Fontana, Cheoah, Calderwood, and Santeetlah Lakes were all visible, lying in quiet repose among the foothills of the Smokies. Good views today require a little exploration of the bald's perimeter and, on a clear day, are worth the effort.

Upon leaving the bald, the trail zigzags down the western flank of the ridge for about three miles before the trail switches back sharply to the left as it enters a rough parcel of ground bearing the marks of a campsite. A post at the switchback indicates campsite 95, the Dalton Branch Backcountry Campsite. This, however, is not the campsite proper. A few feet beyond the switchback, a path crosses a feeder stream and continues one hundred yards to a spacious, gently sloping site above Dalton Branch. The path to the camp continues as a manway to the stateline divide where it meets the original route of the Appalachian Trail descending to Deals Gap.

The trail leading from the campsite is the remnant of an old road. About one mile from the campsite, just after passing along a high bank above a deep gorge carved by Dalton Branch, the western terminus of the Twenty Mile Loop Trail intersects on the left. Wolf Ridge Trail continues as an old railroad grade on a streamside course along Moore Spring Branch. In its last mile the trail crosses the stream five times, with the last three on foot logs. Near the confluence of Moore Spring Branch and Twenty Mile Creek, Wolf Ridge Trail rejoins the Twentymile Trail for an easy walk back to the Twentymile parking area. 🚶🚶

The Best Overnight Hikes in the Great Smoky Mountains was designed and typeset on a Macintosh Quadra using PageMaker software. The text font is Stone serif, with statistical data set in Stone Sans. The display fonts are Copperplate 33bc and Cochin Bold Italic.

This book was designed by Todd Duren and composed in-house at the press.

The paper used in this book is designed for an effective life of at least three hundred years.